A FORGIVING HEART

A BEAUTIFUL LIFE

Mark Baker

ISBN 0-9767929-0-7

First Printing June 2005

Publisher: Hope Ink
Cover Design & Photo: Hope Ink

www.hopeink.net

Printed in the United States of America
Morris Publishing
3212 East Highway 30
Kearney, NE 68847
1-800-650-7888

The prophet Isaiah foretold the coming of Jesus Christ and how God's New Covenant would change everything.

The Spirit of the Sovereign LORD is on me,
because the LORD has anointed me
to preach good news to the poor.
He has sent me to bind up the brokenhearted,
to proclaim freedom for the captives
and release from darkness for the prisoners,

to proclaim the year of the LORD's favor
and the day of vengeance of our God,
to comfort all who mourn,

and provide for those who grieve in Zion—
to bestow on them a crown of beauty
instead of ashes,
the oil of gladness
instead of mourning,
and a garment of praise
instead of a spirit of despair.
They will be called oaks of righteousness,
a planting of the LORD
for the display of his splendor.

Isaiah 61:1-3

CONTENTS

WHO SHOULD READ THIS BOOK?

Read this book if…

You want to understand and experience mercy and grace.

You want to understand how life works.

You struggle with pornography, alcohol, drugs, food, money, etc.

You want a "fair" life.

You struggle with anger.

You struggle with depression.

You struggle with worry and fear.

You care too much about what people think of you.

You want to know and experience true freedom.

You have relationships which are based mainly on *performance*, rather than on grace and mercy.

You are bitter.

Your mother and/or father were bitter and angry.

You struggle in one or more of your relationships.

You want to expose the subtle lies and distortions of the truth which have infiltrated the church.

You want to counsel others.

You struggle to resolve conflict.

You are married.

You are not married.

You want to know God more.

You want to love God more.

You struggle to know love.

You struggle with understanding love.

You struggle with giving love.

You lack hope.

You lack love, joy, peace, patience, kindness…and self-control.

You struggle with insecurity.

You struggle to deal with or overcome the past.

You have been deeply and repeatedly hurt.

You have had a painful life.

You struggle to understand and appreciate pain and suffering.

You have had an ugly life.

You want to change your life.

You want a new life.

You want a beautiful life.

If applied, the truth from God's Word contained in this book will help you grow tremendously in all of these areas.

THE GOOD NEWS

For God so loved the world that he gave his one and only Son, that whoever believes in him shall not perish but have eternal life. For God did not send his Son into the world to condemn the world, but to save the world through him. Whoever believes in him is not condemned, but whoever does not believe stands condemned already because he has not believed in the name of God's one and only Son.

John 3:16-18

Man was created by God in the image of God and lived in paradise. He walked with God and knew God. But Adam and Eve, the first man and woman, doubted God's character and rejected God's Word and provision (Gen 3:1-13). Their sin separated them from God (Gen 3:22-24; Is 59:2) and brought on them the penalty of their sin…*death* (Rom 1:32; 5:16-17; 6:23).

We have all chosen to disobey God and have sinned against Him (Rom 3:23). We have all failed to do what is right. Therefore, because He is a God of justice, we too will experience the penalty for our sin…death, both in our bodies and for eternity (i.e., hell). There is nothing *we* can do to make up for all the wrong things we have done. Our *only* hope is found in the love, grace, and mercy of God.

Because God loves us, He made a way for us to be restored to Him (Rom 5:8). Out of His love and the need to satisfy His justice, He sent His only Son, Jesus, to pay the penalty for our sins (Jn 3:16). Jesus received the punishment that you and I deserve. He died in our place so that we might be forgiven our sin, debt, and penalty. What is more, after three days He rose from the grave so that He would have power over death and life. Now we are able to live with Him forever in heaven.

This pardon cannot be earned, nor is it based on one's worth. It is, however, free to anyone who *believes* in Jesus (Jn 1:12; 3:16), admits their sins (1 Jn 1:9; Ps 32:5), and turns from their sinful ways (Matt 3:8; 1 Thess 1:9). Eternal life is a gift from God that is received by faith despite one's lack of merit and worth (Eph 2:3-9). The forgiveness of our sins is based solely on the character of God and one's faith in Jesus and the work He did on the cross (Phil 3:8-9; Ti 3:4-7).

You too can be saved from the penalty of your sins. If you acknowledge the sin in your life, if you desire to stop your old sinful ways, if you want to turn your life over to Jesus, then pray and ask Him to forgive you of all the sin you have done. The Bible says, "If we confess our sins, he is faithful and just and will forgive us our sins and purify us from all unrighteousness" (1 Jn 1:9).

Say a simple pray like, "Jesus I know that I have sinned against you and deserve the punishment my sins require. I want to stop my old ways and live for you. Please forgive me of all that I have done to hurt you. Please help me as I rely on you to change my life. Show me how to live my life and how to love you. Thank you for loving me, dying for me, and forgiving me."

1

TO FORGIVE OR NOT TO FORGIVE

Frank's childhood was exceptionally painful. Like the experiences of many others, his pain came from within his own home—and that from the hand of a step-parent. His grief tormented him day and night long past his youth. There was seemingly no hope in sight.

"If I could just get married," thought Frank "then I would be able to move on and start a new life." Finally his wedding day arrived. This was his long awaited escape, the turning point of his life. Unfortunately, it would not be a change for the better.

Instead of a new beginning and freedom from the past, the hurt and bitterness came to a head. Frank exploded in volcanic fashion, overflowing with pain and bitterness. The unsuspecting recipient was his beautiful and blameless bride. She was dazed, hurt, and confused, but this was only the beginning.

As much as Frank wanted a new start, something kept his heart and soul shackled to the pain of his distant past. Weeks, months, and years went by without any progress. Hundreds of therapy sessions and tens of thousands of dollars later, his marriage, life, and relationships were even worse than before.

Something inside of him knew the solution to all of his anguish, but, stubbornly, he refused to embrace the cure to his self-described "life's curse." "That's too easy; it's too simple," he argued. "Nobody knows how much pain I've been through! And besides, I am not letting that *%#@% get away with it. It's not fair! He must pay dearly for everything he did to me!"

While the fruit in his life may not convince you, Frank has been a Christian for as long as he can remember. However, he cannot recall ever knowing the peace, joy, and hope that he hears so much about. In fact, every time Frank reads or hears of those things, it makes him doubt God's character a little more. "If God is so good, then why am I so miserable most of the time? How could a loving God allow this to happen to me? Maybe these promises are true for others, but I doubt if they're true for me."

> If God is so good, then why am I so miserable?

> Maybe these promises are true for others, but I doubt if they're true for me.

When Frank came into my office, he knew that my counsel would match the solution of which he was already painfully aware. After talking for a short while, he fully realized that he himself held the keys to his own freedom, joy, and peace—not his step-father, not his mother, not his wife, his children, or his job. Frank would not readily admit it, but deep down he understood that his day-to-day experience was solely dependent upon God and his love and reliance upon Him.

"Yeah, but…," he stubbornly interjected. Everything Frank was hearing was undeniably straight from God's Word, yet he would repeatedly interrupt with "Yeah, but…" If a Christian does not desire to trust in, submit to, and follow God's Word, then what hope is there? This is hell in and of itself!

"Forgiveness!? Yeah, but he doesn't *deserve* forgiveness. Do you have any idea how much pain I have been through?" After a while, Frank realized that he could no longer fight the abundant reality of Scripture. Still, he tried to salvage his losing battle through a compromise. This would be his final stand in his battle with God's Word. "I'll forgive him," Frank said, "but only on one condition—that he come crawling on his hands and knees, begging me to forgive him. Maybe, *maybe* I will forgive him then."

He would try what we so often attempt: Frank would concede some of the Bible's truth, *but only* if he could add stipulations, restrictions, and loop-holes to God's perfect Word and design. Frank had a pattern of trying to fit God's Word into his desires, rather than conforming his desires and life to God.

In addition to this, Frank knew his proposal was an almost certain impossibility in that he had cut off any contact with his step-father over a decade ago. Frank had no idea where his step-father was, or if he was even alive. There was certainly no way of contacting him, even if Frank had had the desire to do so.

By leaving himself a way out, the true condition of Frank's heart was revealed. What kind of faith, hope, love, and commitment to God did he really have? "If … maybe … then …" "Yeah, but …" While he occasionally listened to suggestions, Frank was proud of the fact that he lived his life according to his terms, his desires, and his will. We both knew that if Frank were ever actually face-to-face with his step-father, he would undoubtedly rely on the escape clause that he had inserted into God's unconditional command. Was Frank's hope in God and His Word, or was it in other people and changing circumstances? Was he pursuing happiness or holiness? Frank's kingdom or God's kingdom?

Frank gave me a long list of areas he wanted help with: addictions, misery, lust, depression, anger, moodiness, worry, fear, poor relationships (especially his relationship with God), manic episodes, paranoia, loneliness, despair, his horrible marriage, the destruction he infects his kids with … the list went on and on. But was he willing to do whatever it took to change all of this? There was hope! There were answers! He could change. But not if he was unwilling.

The problem was not so much what had happened in the past, although there was no denying that horrific pain. The real crisis was how Frank was handling it. The problem

"Yeah, but he doesn't deserve forgiveness."

"Resentment kills."

Job 5:2

"Judgment without mercy will be shown to anyone who has not been merciful. Mercy triumphs over judgment!"

James 2:13

A Beautiful Life

was his unyielding and unchanged heart. So many years as a Christian and yet he was still struggling mightily to experience even a hint of peace, joy, hope, love, transformation, and even God Himself. This was definitely not God's will for Frank—as it is not His will for any of us.

Yet, Frank had always known the answer. Even so, the more he learned, the more he dug his heels in. While he may not have grasped all that made up the solution, he repeatedly refused to trust and obey God's desire and design in those things that he *did* understand.

Ultimately, however foolish it may sound, he wanted to dwell on the injustice, offenses, and pain of the past more than he desired to go through the uncomfortable, challenging, yet beautiful and freeing process of forgiveness. Nothing could ever change Frank's history, but forgiveness would transport him out of the pain of the past and into present freedom and peace. Yet Frank mistakenly believed he "needed" revenge, justice, fairness, happiness, etc.—all the things that his flesh and the world told him he needed.

However, God saw, as He does with all of us, a different need. What Frank really needed was a changed heart. He needed to know God and His abundant love and grace. He needed to trust God and His Word. Frank needed to fully appreciate his own undeserved, unfair gift from God. He needed to repent, conform to, and imitate Christ, especially through forgiveness. He needed to humble himself and submit to God, and His Word, plan, and will for his life. In all of this, Frank needed to turn his "Yeah, but…" into "Yes, Lord!"

So, what was the outcome? What did Frank decide? After thoroughly going over all of God's truth, design, and desire for him, after exposing and expunging the lies of the world and his psychologists, after answering all of his questions and resolving his "yeah, but…" objections, Frank said to me, "*Yeah*, you're absolutely right. I agree with what you're saying one hundred percent. *But*, I don't want what you are offering. Thanks, but no thanks."

What good is your will if it is against God's will? What good is God's Word without faith and obedience? What good is wisdom if you cherish the world and its folly? What good is pain if you don't learn and grow from it? What good is truth if you do not trust it? What is love without commitment, actions, and truth? What good is God to you if you don't need Him, know Him, love Him, or hope in Him? How much hope is to be found in dwelling on and living in the past? What good is the key to freedom if you insist on remaining enslaved? What is life without forgiveness?

While Frank's experience and his resulting stubbornness may sound rare or extreme, it is actually quite common. Although the degree of severity may vary, Frank's type of experience is all too familiar within the body of Christ, not to mention society as a whole. I would conservatively estimate that at least eighty percent of those whom I counsel have a significant issue with unforgiveness and anger, while one hundred percent of them could grow immensely in grace, mercy, and love.

"I desire mercy, not sacrifice."

Matthew 9:13

He needed to turn his "Yeah, but…" into "Yes, Lord!"

"When my heart was grieved and my spirit embittered, I was senseless and ignorant; I was a brute beast before you."

Psalm 73:21-22

As Christians, we have *all* struggled to forgive at one time or another. The foreign concepts of grace and mercy are not the only hurdles we must overcome. For many of us, like Frank, it is a matter of our heart and our will before God. Who is going to win? Who is going to lose? Ultimately *you* determine the outcome.

It is my hope and belief that the more we know, appreciate, and cherish God's love, grace, mercy, and Word, the more willing we will be to freely forgive, and the more beautiful our lives will be. This, of course, requires time and practice. First, we must spend a significant amount of *time*, even sacrificially, in reading, meditating on, absorbing, and valuing God's gracious love. The more time we spend doing these things, the more we will delight in the reality, the beauty, and the truth of God's Word. This, in turn, will transform our hearts and lives. Second, we must put what we learn into practice. And finally, no matter what happens, we need to remember that each of us, not other people or circumstances, hold the keys to our own life and freedom; and, further, that the keys only work when we trust God and follow through on His design and desire.

Imagine driving along with a friend. You are on a long trip and you trust this person enough to be your navigator. You come to a fork in the road and your traveling companion tells you to turn left when you should have turned right. It does not take long before you realize you have turned into a dead end.

What do you do now? How do you respond? How will this impact the rest of your trip? Are you angry with your navigator with whom you have entrusted so much? Do you pull over for a while and, in no uncertain terms, enlighten him as to what an idiot he is and how mad he has made you? Do you go into great detail as to how any dimwit would have known to turn right?

Or, are you painfully aware of your own weaknesses, knowing quite well that everyone makes mistakes, even silly ones like this? Do you simply turn your car around and get back on the right path? Do you have compassion for your friend who may feel terribly embarrassed over his mistake and this unnecessary delay? Do you see your friend as far more important than this trip itself? Do you remember a time when you did something similar with the results being far worse? Do you see the opportunity to encourage, love, and give grace to your friend—in the same way that you would want to be done for you?

There are no flawless navigators, no flawless drivers. Anyone can make a wrong turn. And in life, each and every one of us has misread a map, gotten lost, and misdirected or offended those we know. Everyone on earth has been steered off course by others, be it maliciously or accidentally.

Unfortunately, many people are stuck in the very same dead end into which they turned years ago. Why is that? Do they have no choice? Are they at the mercy of the person who misled them? Is the navigator keeping them there? Is there any hope?

It seems that many people know the way out, and can even see it, but they refuse to leave. Instead, they are consumed with the offense of the wrong turn. Often they would

Paul said:

"I have learned the secret of being content in any and every situation."

Philippians 4:12

Joseph said:

"You intended to harm me, but God intended it for good."

Genesis 50:20

rather park the car and yell at the person that misled them. Or they may sit there silently, squeezing the steering wheel, while burning on the inside as they rehash the wrong turn over and over.

Maybe they want to blame other misfortunes in life on this event and/or the navigator. Others are consumed with informing anyone who can hear what a jerk, what an imbecile, their navigator is. Some even drive around and around in circles, increasing their angst and bitterness with every revolution.

Sometimes the navigator, the responsible party, may stick around and try to make things right. He may even admit his fault and try to correct the problem. But what can he do if the driver refuses to get back on the right road? Now it is the driver, not the navigator, who controls the outcome of the trip and the correction of the mistake. Eventually, after enough time, dismissal, and even mistreatment, the traveling companion will usually move on, leaving the hopeless person and situation behind.

However ridiculous this stubborn resistance may sound, we have all been there—in either role. Some of us eventually move on and are able to enjoy life, while others never get out alive. To which camp do you tend to belong? If you feel like your life is trapped in a dead end, what are you *willing* to do to get out? Are you trying to hold others hostage with you, or do you desire freedom and grace for all?

How silly it is when we refuse to move on! How foolish to miss out on so much of life, all because someone else did something wrong. Does God want our lives to come to a screeching halt? Or does He want us to learn, grow, and move past these unfortunate episodes? Far too many people are spinning their wheels in the muck of the past. Can they forgive? Can they move on, no matter how much they have been hurt? God says *yes*. What do *you* say about your own offenses and hurts?

The undeniable reality is that everyone has been hurt. In fact, everyone has been *deeply* hurt. Life, true life, the abundant life, is not a matter of *if* or *how much* you will be hurt, but of love, grace, forgiveness, and God's glory *in the midst of hurt*.

Those who stumble over past hurts, those who have made a dead end their regular abode miss out on much of life and on God's purposes for them. What is more, they negatively impact and stain others in such an ugly way. Instead of bringing light, joy, love, hope, and grace to other people, as is their calling by God, they spread the venom of unforgiveness and the torture and death which result from constant demands for "fairness" and fulfillment of their fleshly desires.

The good news is that it does not have to be this way. *Forgiveness is the key to life*: both life eternal, as well as the abundant life that Jesus promised here on earth. But giving mercy and grace is not just something you *do*; it is more a matter of who you *are*. It must proceed from the right kind of heart, a heart transformed by God and His abundant love. Unlimited change, love, and fruit lie before you. Life does not depend on those who have hurt you; the life you experience is determined by your faithfulness to God's design and desires.

If you feel like your life is trapped in a dead end, what are you willing to do to get out?

Forgiveness is the key to a beautiful life.

Life, true life, the abundant life, is not a matter of IF or HOW MUCH you will be hurt, but of love, grace, forgiveness, and God's glory IN THE MIDST OF HURT.

Let's consider another example, a woman named Mary. Compared to the early days of Mary's life, Frank's childhood was a walk in the park. In fact, it is difficult not to weep when hearing just a fraction of the mistreatment and heinous crimes committed against her.

Yet, even with the difference in severity, Mary's dilemma was essentially the same as Frank's. That is, would she remain in the past and continuously re-live all of the pain? Would she give up control of her life to the very person who hurt her? Would she continue to go around and around in the dead end where she was misled? Or would she, no matter how uncomfortable and difficult it was, choose to forgive and be set free?

Thankfully, the response of Mary's heart was to forgive. While her choice was far easier said than done, Mary's trust in God was more than she needed (e.g., His grace, power, love, truth, wisdom) to go against her flesh and the world's thinking.

Did she succeed because of her intelligence? Was it because she was a good, righteous, or strong person? No, in fact, it was because Mary was all too familiar with weakness, brokenness, hardship, being crushed, and even her own sin that she was so able to appreciate grace and mercy. Therefore, she chose to walk in God's love and not in the way of the flesh.

Mary's formerly unfathomable pain has now become invaluable. It has taught her the priceless lesson that her hope and her life are not in this world. What is more, she has learned the futility of putting her hope in the performance of people or even in herself. Her own fleeting happiness and being treated well by others are no longer the pursuits of her life.

What she now longs for is far higher, far greater, far deeper, more real, and much more beautiful. In fact, all of the anguish she has endured has served Mary quite well. Ultimately, it has pushed her more and more into the arms of the One who will never let her down. Now she is storing up treasures in heaven and learning to trust and obey God's design and desire, no matter what happens to her.

Today Mary is free. She is not chained to her past. She has an incredible marriage, a godly husband, and wonderful children. She faithfully serves in ministry and is able to bring incredible light and love to others who have also been deeply hurt. Mary is known for her faithfulness, love, peace, and joy, and not for her pain or grievances. *Mary has a beautiful life!*

Where would Mary be without forgiveness? How different would her impact on those around her be (e.g., Frank's impact)? What kind of man would she have married? Would she have given her kids a similar experience to the one she had? More importantly, how different would her impact on eternity and the kingdom of God be?

Can forgiveness make that big of a difference? Can a forgiving heart be the distinction between an ugly existence and a beautiful life? The answer is yes—more than you can imagine. While the stories of Frank and Mary are prime examples of the contrast between forgiveness and unforgiveness, there are countless others who have either been

Giving mercy and grace is not just something you DO; it is more a matter of who you ARE.

Can forgiveness make that big of a difference?

Can a forgiving heart be the distinction between an ugly existence and a beautiful life?

The answer is yes—more than you can imagine.

Jesus said:

"Blessed are the merciful."

Matthew 5:7

destroyed by bitterness, or who have been radically blessed and changed through grace and mercy.

Today Mary's sister, who knows first hand of her torment, is amazed that Mary turned out the way she did. Mary's reply to her amazement is simple: "What's so shocking about choosing not to live a life of torment?" she asks humbly. "It was hard at first, but I simply chose the *easier path*. I chose to forgive and live. 'Blessed are the merciful.' I am truly blessed."

Chances are you know a lot of people like Frank. Their past pain, current misery, and lack of life come through in most, if not all, of your encounters with them. Their sharp tongues and biting words quickly spread their pain and grief to others.

On the other hand, you may not realize how many people like Mary are in your life. They too have been deeply hurt, but you would probably never know it. They are not consumed, controlled, or limited by their past painful experiences. Complaints of unfairness and injustice are not continually on their lips. Instead, hope, joy, and godly wisdom mark their words and life.

Sadly, if you have lived long enough, then you personally know several people who have wrecked their lives and relationships on the jagged rocks of stubborn unforgiveness. However, it does not have to end that way. There is yet still hope. In spite of everything, they can have life and life to the full. They can have beauty for ashes.

What about you? Do you struggle with forgiveness? Do you resist or refuse to give mercy? Is there pain from your past that is eating you up on the inside? Is there something or someone that you just can't forgive? Is your experience in life controlled by what others do or have done to you? If so, what follows can transform your life. But only if you are willing.

Like Frank, not everyone *wants* to get past his or her past. For them, it is not a matter of "know-how," ability, or the level of pain. They simply refuse. They are more than willing to stay in their misery. Jesus encountered just such a person in His earthly ministry. Therefore, He had to ask a seemingly obvious, yet necessary, question. This question is one that each of us needs to answer as well.

> When Jesus saw him lying there and learned that he had been in this condition for a long time, he asked him,
>
> *"Do you want to get well?"*
>
> John 5:6, italics added

What about you?

Is there something or someone that you just can't forgive?

Do YOU want to get well?

2

YOUR GREATEST NEED

Never has something been more necessary, more valuable, more indispensable, more vital, more important, more life changing, while at the same time so disdained, so disregarded, so unappreciated, so misunderstood, and so bungled. Forgiveness is essential to our existence, to our relationships, to eternity, to love, to knowing God, and yet, to our shame, it is exceedingly neglected and even outright rejected.

Forgiveness is the difference, literally, between life and death, heaven and hell. It is, therefore, *your greatest need*. Knowing and living a life of grace and mercy will not only alter your eternal destination, it will thoroughly transform your heart, relationships, and life. It is usually the difference between living life abundantly or enduring a life of misery.

Not only is forgiveness lacking in our world but, ashamedly, within the body of Christ as well. What is more, unforgiveness, as you will see, has far greater destructive consequences for the Christian than for the non-believer.

Because our lives are completely dependent upon forgiveness, we need to understand it as wholly and completely as we can. This requires a great deal of *biblical* understanding to make up for our huge lack of awareness, comprehension, appreciation, and fulfillment of this incredible life-giving act. Because of the magnitude of the grace, mercy, love, and blessings that go into forgiveness, all of us, no matter what our level of spiritual maturity, have volumes of growth before us.

Who knows more about forgiveness than the Forgiver? Who can impart more wisdom concerning grace than the One who sits on the throne of grace? Jesus, who is forgiveness, clearly and abundantly lives, breathes, demonstrates, and imparts all of the essentials of forgiveness. In Jesus' life here on earth the Bible records two stories regarding the impact of forgiveness and unforgiveness: one parable and one real, one ugly and one beautiful, in order to revolutionize your way of thinking and, more importantly, to transform your heart. Both stories will be thoroughly examined here.

Much of the world's thinking, ways of life, and "wisdom" will be exposed throughout this book. What will be revealed are the usual suspects that get us into trouble in the first place. They are the probably the culprits that not only *started* our problems, but also continue to keep us locked in darkness and torment. Therefore, these ideas and desires must be

FORGIVENESS:

Not holding the sin, offense, debt against the offender.

MERCY:

Not getting what you deserve (i.e., hell).

GRACE:

Getting what you do not deserve (i.e., heaven).

uncovered and demolished by the power and light of God's Word if we are to know truth, freedom, forgiveness, and God Himself.

The destructive impact of man's "wisdom" is one of the reasons why there will be an abundance of Scripture referenced throughout this book. These verses are well worth the effort of looking up, knowing, and applying to your life.

Because the concepts and realities of grace and mercy are so deep, so life transforming, so indispensable, and so foreign to our flesh, you may need to read and re-read this book several times. And as you read, please spend plenty of time "examining the Scriptures" to verify all of these things for yourself (Acts 17:11).

Let's illustrate the intricacy of forgiveness by comparing it to child rearing. Some may look at raising children and think, "What's the big deal? You feed them, clothe them, and give them some shelter. What's so hard about that?" While there is *some* truth here, this way of thinking is not only appalling, but misses the whole point and, if applied, would do serious damage. With this lack of understanding we would never appreciate the glorious fruit and beauty that comes from the high calling of parenting.

An abundance of wisdom, love, sacrifice, faith, patience, selflessness, serving, truth, strength, perseverance, discipline, etc, all coming from the right kind of heart, go into the proper and best way of raising kids. If you have children, you already know this.

These godly realities are true with forgiveness as well. If we think that merely saying, "I forgive you," is all that goes into forgiveness, especially when deeply hurt, we will experience much needless heartache and destruction. The same wisdom, love, sacrifice, and the right kind of heart are needed to understand, value, and fulfill God's desired forgiveness. If you have ever truly forgiven a painful offense, you know this all to well.

Therefore, we will be extremely thorough in our attempt to learn and live out this vital way of life—our utmost need. Some things in this book may seem repetitious; this is not a mistake, but rather, a valuable and essential tool in learning this supreme reality.

The focus here will not be on past wounds and offenses. The assumption is that you have been hurt in the past. In fact, you have probably been deeply hurt, betrayed, and offended several times throughout your life. I do not want to minimize the severe pain of the past. Rather, my desire is to focus on dealing with your heartache in the right way so that you can be rid of it for good.

As you read this book, you will undoubtedly think of more than one person who could benefit from the blessing of forgiveness. But please try to concentrate on thoroughly applying these life-transforming realities to your life first. Take all the time you need to absorb and appreciate this vital concept and life-giving reality.

> The world's "wisdom" must be uncovered and demolished by the power and light of God's Word.

> If we think that merely saying, "I forgive you," is all that goes into forgiveness ... we will experience much needless heartache and destruction.

3

DAY OF RECKONING

Matthew 18:23-35

Therefore, the kingdom of heaven is like a king who wanted to settle accounts with his servants. As he began the settlement, a man who owed him ten thousand talents was brought to him.

verses 23-24

Have you ever had a horrible feeling of dread come over you? Maybe it was brought on by an impending visit to the doctor. Or maybe a late night phone call. Perhaps as a child you were summoned to the principal's office. Maybe you were called before your boss or a judge. How about being pulled over by the police? Of course, that sickening feeling is far worse when you know you are guilty of something.

The servant in Jesus' parable finds himself in an utterly dreadful situation. The encounters listed above are nothing compared to what is about to happen to this servant. He is on the verge of reaping the ugly consequences for his heinous crimes.

What do you suppose is going through his mind? Is he fearful? Is he merely thinking of an excuse to finagle his way out of his predicament? Is he truly sorry for what he has done? Does he have a patsy to blame everything on? Will he repent?

In Jesus' day, ten thousand talents was not exactly petty cash. This would be equal to approximately $30,000,000 to $50,000,000 today (some even estimate this debt could have been up to one billion dollars!). Either way, this was an insurmountable debt, one which the servant could never come close to repaying.

How does a servant accumulate $10,000 in losses—let alone a $50,000,000 shortfall? A person would have to be intentionally and aggressively corrupt in order to achieve this level of deficit. This servant was nothing but a thief, and not a very good one at that. His generous master had entrusted him with so much, yet the servant repaid this kindness and loyalty with sickening betrayal.

> How does a servant accumulate $10,000 in losses —let alone a $50,000,000 shortfall?

A crucial life or death realization can be found here. As sinners, we are just like this servant with our debt, ineptitude, and crookedness. We too are extraordinarily incompetent and corrupt in keeping our Master's desires. Our footing is equally ominous; you and I can never come close to paying off our mammoth deficit.

Furthermore, our liability swells with each feeble attempt to make amends. It seems that the more we strive, the more we fall short of our Master's standard and desire. The amount of our sin (debt) is to such an extent that our finite minds will never fully grasp the colossal degree of our separation from God.

The scariest part for many is that we, like the servant, will stand in the presence of God and give Him an account for all that He has given us (Heb 4:12-13). Will you "have to" or "get to" give an account to God? What will your experience be like? Will you be greeted with, "Well done, good and faithful servant" (Matt 25:23)? Or will you make it to heaven, "but only as one escaping through the flames" (1 Cor 3:14)?

As sinners, we are just like this servant with our debt, ineptitude, and crookedness.

- What similarities do you find between the servant and yourself?

- Are you looking forward to or dreading your face-to-face encounter with Christ? Why?

- What is your view of God? Is He a condemning judge? A being who is unapproachable and distant? Someone who is there to answer your requests/prayers?

- How does your view of God affect your relationships with others and your ability and desire to forgive?

4

BAD NEWS LEADS TO THE GOOD NEWS

Matthew 18:23-35

Since he was not able to pay, the master ordered that he and his wife and his children and all that he had be sold to repay the debt.

verse 25

Whether we realize or not, there are tremendous consequences to our actions (Gen 3; Gal 6:7-8; Heb 12:16-17; Rev 20:15). While some people may seem to unfairly get away with their heinous actions (Job 21:7-16; Ps 37; 73; Jer 12:1-2; Mal 3:14-15), there is a steep and dreadful penalty to pay for our debt as sinners (Rom 6:23).

Rarely do we fully appreciate the magnitude of our debt and the truly terrifying consequences we deserve. As a result, God's gift is equally unappreciated or missed altogether. In addition, for many of us, painful consequences and God's displeasure fail to deter us from doing what we want.

What do you think you deserve? Respect? Equality? Love? Security? Esteem? Your fair share? Nothing? Everything? While all of these are common answers to this question, the painful reality is that you overwhelmingly deserve death! (Rom 3:23, 5:12, 6:23) Why else would Jesus die for you unless death is the penalty for sinners? (See Jn 3:16; 15:13; Rom 5:6-10, 12, 17.)

This unpleasant, unnerving, yet precious understanding is the first step to salvation…realizing what you truly deserve because of the hideousness and enormity of your sin…and therefore realizing your *absolute need*, beyond measure, for a Savior. "Blessed are the poor in spirit, for theirs is the kingdom of heaven" (Matt 5:3).

When we comprehend the horrible condition of our hearts, how repulsive our sin is to a holy God, and the inestimable separation between us and God, we set the table to appreciate what kind of God would love us, die for us, and grant us eternal life—given the atrocious and evil nature of our hearts and behavior (Rom 5:5-8; Col 1:21-22; Ti 3:3-7). This grief results in life. "Blessed are those who mourn, for they will be comforted. Blessed are the meek, for they will inherit the earth" (Matt 5:4-5).

> There is a steep and dreadful penalty to pay for our debt as sinners.

> The painful reality is that we overwhelmingly deserve death!

On the other hand, if we don't humble ourselves so that we can see the true condition of our hearts, then we fail to see our utmost need (Eph 1:18). If we don't acknowledge our sin (1 Jn 1:9), if we have no contrition (Ps 51:17; Prov 28:13), if we do not see our need (Matt 23; Mk 1:15), if we do not long for our highest need, *then we must conclude that we don't need a Savior* (Jn 12:40; Mk 4:12; Lk 7:36-50; 18:9-14).

If we do not have a Savior, then we do not have salvation. Not only will we miss out on eternal life, but we will never experience the abundant life that the Savior promises (John 10:10). "Blessed are those who hunger and thirst for righteousness, for they will be filled" (Matt 5:6).

If we are basically good, if we are *worthy* of God's love and salvation, if we are "not that bad," if we are concerned about and live for ideas like "high *self*-esteem," then we are blind, we are still lost, we do not know the truth, we will not know grace (there is no need), and we will not truly know, love, and appreciate God and His gift of salvation (Matt 13:14-17). "This is the one I esteem: he who is *humble* and *contrite* in spirit, and trembles at My word" (Is 66:2, italics added; see also Ps 34:18; 51:17; Is 57:15).

Again, the primary and essential understanding needed, in order to have, know, and truly enjoy life, is to grasp the true condition and level of sin in our hearts and lives (Matt 5:3-5; Lk 18:9-14; Rom 3:10-18; Is 6:5-7). We cannot rely on what others see, how we feel, what the world says, or on what we want to believe, but on the truth, on what God knows our hearts to be.

How does God see and describe our hearts?

> The Lord saw how great man's wickedness on the earth had become, and that every inclination of the thoughts of his heart was *only evil all the time*.
>
> Genesis 6:5, italics added

> The hearts of men, moreover, are *full of evil* and there is *madness* in their hearts while they live, and afterward they join the dead.
>
> Ecclesiastes 9:3, italics added

> The heart is *deceitful above all things* and beyond cure. Who can understand it?
>
> Jeremiah 17:9, italics added

> For from within, out of men's hearts, come evil thoughts, sexual immorality, theft, murder, adultery, greed, malice, deceit, lewdness, envy, slander, arrogance and folly.
>
> Mark 7:21-22

How does God depict the desires of our sinful nature? They are: lustful (2 Pet 2:18), evil (Col 3:5), deceitful (Eph 4:22), corrupt (2 Pet 2:10), and contrary to God and His desires (Gal 5:17).

If we do not have a Savior, then we do not have salvation.

In order to have, know, and truly enjoy life, we must grasp the true condition and level of sin in our hearts and lives.

However uncomfortable and painful this realization might be, no matter what it does to your self-esteem or self-worth, it ushers in hope, salvation, grace, freedom, love, joy, peace, and blessing *if* and *when* you humble yourself before God, repent, and entrust your life to Him.

This ugly picture of our hearts is like a doctor's life-saving diagnosis. It may not be pleasant being told you have a deadly disease, but without the truth and accuracy of this information you would surely die from your woeful condition.

But with a correct diagnosis there is hope. We know precisely what our problem is. Now we know we need a cure. We need the Savior! With this awareness we need to humbly go before Him and cry out for undeserved forgiveness.

Without true humility in the presence of God, how much hope do you have? That is why Scripture says:

> *God opposes the proud but gives grace to the humble.* Submit yourselves, then, to God. Resist the devil, and he will flee from you. Come near to God and He will come near to you. Wash your hands, you sinners, and purify your hearts, you double-minded. Grieve, mourn and wail. Change your laughter to mourning and your joy to gloom. *Humble yourselves before the Lord, and He will lift you up.*
>
> James 4:6-10, italics added

> He has showed you, O man, what is good. And what does the Lord require of you? *To act justly and to love mercy and to walk humbly with your God.*
>
> Micah 6:8, italics added

With a correct diagnosis there is hope. We know precisely what our problem is.

- On a scale of 0 to 100, how would you rate the goodness of your heart apart from God? What does your rating indicate about you?

- How would you describe the desires of *your* sinful nature?

- What do *you* deserve?

- For what, specifically, do you mourn? (e.g., your sin, not getting your own way, being mistreated by others, your weaknesses, "unfairness," your separation from God?)

- Would it be safe to say that those who know you well would describe you as "humble" or "poor in spirit"? Why or why not? Would they describe you as "stubborn" or "prideful"? Why?

- What do you *need*?

- Do you know Jesus? What might have to change in order for you to know Him better?

5

A HEART REVEALED

Matthew 18:23-35

The servant fell on his knees before him. "Be patient with me," he begged, "and I will pay back everything."

verse 26

Given our horrible sin and separation from God, what is our only hope? Higher self-esteem? To work harder? Better luck? To become a better person? More self-worth? More time? To pay off the debt *ourselves*? A ten-point plan to visualize success and maximize our abilities? *No!*

Our *one* and *only* hope is to receive mercy from the Master. Notice that our solitary hope is the extreme opposite of the world's thinking and "wisdom." Our fate rests solely on the character of God (and not in our worth). There is absolutely nothing we can do to be absolved from our crimes except to trust in His character (Lk 23:42-43; Eph 2:8-9; 2 Tim 1:9).

It is possible, even probable because of his later actions (see Matt 3:8-10; Jas 2:26), that the servant was not completely sincere in pleading for mercy. What was his real motive? Did he truly humble himself? Was there any repentance? Was there godly sorrow or worldly sorrow (see 2 Cor 7:10-11)? Was his hope in the character of the master or in his ability and/or worth? His fruit reveals the root (see Lk 8:11-15). A root is the true motive, hope, and belief.

When confronted with the magnitude of his gross incompetence, failings, and corruption, the servant reveals his heart's true condition as he falls far short of surrendering his pride. Stubbornness and pride are the inseparable friends of death and destruction. They are always accompanied by ruined relationships and the absence of life.

The focus is still on himself (i.e., pride), and not on the wonderful nature of the master (humility), as evidenced by his statement, *"I will* pay back everything" (see Is 14:12-15). When your attention is on yourself and what you are getting, then you cannot focus on God or others. It is impossible to focus on two separate things at the same time. You might as well try taking pride in your humility!

> Our fate rests solely on the character of God (not in our worth).

> Do you experience godly sorrow or worldly sorrow?

While what he needs is mercy, the servant is still focused on and putting hope in his ability to somehow become "worthy." Ironically, this is the same "ability" and prideful character that got him into so much trouble in the first place! He still believes in himself. "He who trusts in himself is a fool" (Prov 28:26). This delusion always sacrifices trust in and love for God. "But he who trusts in the Lord will prosper" (Prov 28:25). This failure to humble himself will come back to haunt him. It always does.

> Since they did not know the righteousness that comes from God and *sought to establish their own*, they did not submit to God's righteousness.
>
> Romans 10:3, italics added

> But whatever was to my profit I now consider loss for the sake of Christ. What is more, I consider everything a loss compared to the surpassing greatness of knowing Christ Jesus my Lord, for whose sake I have lost all things. I consider them rubbish, that I may gain Christ and be found in him, *not having a righteousness of my own* that comes from the law, but that which is through faith in Christ–the righteousness *that comes from God and is by faith*.
>
> Philippians 3:7-9, italics added

This failure to humble himself will come back to haunt him. It always does.

- Where do you tend to put your hope?
  (Good circumstances? Money? Your abilities? God? Others satisfying your "emotional needs"?
  A comfortable life? Material possessions? Your looks? Respect from others?)

- What does the fruit in your life reveal concerning your true motives?

- How much importance and emphasis do you place on the unpopular realities of repentance and humility? Why?

- Where in life has your failure to humble yourself come back to haunt you?

- How can *you* tell the difference between "worldly sorrow" and "godly sorrow"?

- How much does your stubbornness and pride influence your relationships?
  Do these characteristics ever add to or enhance your life and relationships? Why or why not?

6

THE MERCIFUL HEART

Matthew 18:23-35

The servant's master took pity on him, canceled the debt and let him go.

verse 27

Because of the severity and prevalence of this problem it bears repeating: as Christians, we often fail to realize, appreciate, and remember what an incredible gift we have received from God. We easily forget that not only do we not deserve this gift, but that we also deserve the wages of our actions (sin)…*death*! We deserve to experience God's wrath being poured out on us for all eternity. "We were by nature objects of wrath" (Eph 2:3).

Understanding the reality of what we truly deserve is the opportunity of a lifetime. It is the foundation of a grateful heart. Yet, failing to appreciate this truth is usually the first wrong turn we make after being so generously and graciously blessed.

Nevertheless, in spite of what we truly merit, God took pity on us, cancelled our colossal debt, and set us free (only for those who truly believe). He gave grace and mercy, not because we deserved it, *but because it is God's character to do so*. "But when the kindness and love of God our Savior appeared, He saved us, not because of righteous things we had done, but because of His mercy" (Ti 3:4-5).

Forgiveness is always subject to the offended person's character, not the worthiness of the offender. We perpetually get this fact backward, especially when it comes to our forgiving others. "But because of *his great love* for us, God, who is *rich in mercy*, made us alive with Christ *even when we were dead in transgressions*—it is by *grace* you have been saved" (Eph 2:4-5, italics added). Living in grace and mercy is far more important and pleasing to God than satisfying our elusive cravings for fairness, justice, or revenge.

We are not worthy of His love—far from it. The Bible says, "All have turned away, they have together become worthless" (Rom 3:12; see also Rom 3:10-18; 2 Kings 17:15). Nevertheless, God, based solely on His character, chooses to love us, *despite our extreme unworthiness*.

> Forgiveness is always subject to the offended person's character, not the worthiness of the offender.

The more worthy we feel, the less we know, experience, and appreciate God's love, grace, mercy, and the joy of our salvation! If we are worthy, then there is no need for grace and mercy! " 'God opposes the proud but gives grace to the humble.' Humble yourselves, therefore, under God's mighty hand, that he may lift you up in due time" (1 Pet 5:5-6).

Our penalty is very real. It did not just disappear. Someone had to pay this enormous price. There is always a cost to forgiveness; however the remaining balance is paid by the forgiver, not the offender. This is another sacrifice on top of the original offense/debt. It costs us nothing to be forgiven by God, but it cost Jesus the ultimate price, and more.

This "unfair" reality is precisely why many struggle with and even refuse to forgive. Even though their current standing in life is based solely on mercy, many believers fail to transition from the "Fairness Doctrine" to a heart overflowing with mercy and grace.

Bitter Christians are stuck in conformity to the world's doctrine and the desires of the flesh. This is a direct result of their failure to be transformed by God's loving character, indwelling powerful Spirit, and exceedingly generous nature.

When your hope is in this world and its "wisdom," you are limited by, and bound to, this world and its ugly existence and experiences (e.g., worry, bitterness, despair, depression; see 2 Pet 1:4). You consume and are consumed by the world's pollution and corruption. However, when your hope is in God and His promises (Ps 119:32), you are set free to enjoy life, while overflowing with love, joy, hope, and peace.

The pursuit of "fairness" in our fallen world is truly "chasing after the wind." On the other hand, living a life in pursuit of God's glory in the face of unfairness results in a beautiful life. This is the life that pleases God. In this quest, we enjoy grace, mercy, and love again and again, all at the expense of bitterness, despair, and unhappiness. The mission for fairness reverses this experience.

The burning questions that the bitter believer lives his life by are, "What am I getting?" and "How am I being treated?" rather than "What am I giving?" (Acts 20:35; Matt 5:42) and "How am I loving others?" (Matt 5:43-47; Jn 15:12).

His heart's desire is fixated on what is seen (temporary gratification, fairness, pleasure, and comfort; see Lk 8:14; 2 Tim 3:1-4), rather than on what is unseen: God's eternal glory and kingdom (2 Cor 4:16-18). His hope tends to be in the dismal performance of sinful man (Ps 6:11, 108:12), to the exclusion of God's unending and perfect love (Ps 62; Rom 1:25; 1 Jn 4:7-21). While our demands are often made under the guise of "fairness," it is really about getting what we want ("I want to get my fair share!").

What it is the solution? What can you do? How can you change? Simply put, do the opposite of what the world wants and your flesh demands. Captivate yourself with the bounty of God's graciousness. Immerse yourself in thankfulness, adoration, and praise. Rivet your gaze onto His kingdom and glory. Check the fruit in your life. It will reveal what, and who, you are focused on and living for.

> If we are worthy, then there is no need for grace and mercy!

> Many believers fail to transition from the "Fairness Doctrine" to a heart overflowing with mercy and grace.

> Because the act of forgiveness is humbling, selfless, sacrificial, and loving, it takes exceptional character to carry out.

In order to forgive others, we need to fully understand and appreciate the reality of who pays the debt in the transaction of forgiveness. In order to fulfill true forgiveness, we need to have the same heart and attitude as Jesus has toward us. Again, the forgiver always pays the cost.

Because this fact is exceedingly unfair, at least in the world's thinking, it requires a remarkable heart. Because the act of forgiveness is humbling, selfless, sacrificial, and loving, it takes exceptional character to carry out. This kind of character can only come from a heart that is more and more changed by the grace and power of God into the image of Jesus (2 Cor 3:18, 4:7; Rom 8:29, 12:1-2).

"But God demonstrates his own love for us in this: While we were still sinners, Christ died for us" (Rom 5:8). Jesus displayed His overall divine nature by coming to earth (humility and love), suffering horrifically ("unfairly"), dying for us (more unfairness, yet satisfying justice/our debt through the greatest love ever known), living again (His infinite power), and opening the door for our forgiveness (despite our lack of merit and all because of His divine and perfect character).

What parts of your character are displayed by your level of forgiveness? Pride? Love? Stubbornness? Compassion? Ungratefulness? Self-centeredness? Graciousness? Demands for "fairness"? Eternal perspective and desire? Fleshly blindness and pursuit of temporary gratification?

What aspects of your character are exposed to others when you are in the midst of conflict? Would they describe you as humble? Always right and never wrong? A "peacemaker" or an appeaser? A perpetual victim? Manipulative? You always say, "Yeah, but..." You confess and take responsibility for your actions? Selfish or godly? Critical or gracious? Forgiving or bitter? You always find a way to avoid dealing with conflict and difficulty? You focus on your "rights" and fairness at the expense of others, resolving the conflict, and glorifying God?

Choosing to forgive, out of faith in, and love for, God, is the *perfect opportunity* to change the undesired characteristics of your heart. Yet, if you refuse this divine opportunity, you dig deeper holes in your character and life experience. You invite more fruit of darkness rather than light and freedom.

The conflicts, offenses, and betrayals in your life are not to be avoided, but are, instead, divine appointments to love God, love others, and conform to the image of Christ? How often do you truly meet God on these occasions? How often does your sinful nature have a preventable and needless growth spurt? Are you more often found on your knees humbly before God, or standing stiff-necked, pounding your fists—demanding that you get your way?

> What aspects of your character are exposed to others when you are in the midst of conflict?

> Choosing to forgive, out of faith in, and love for, God, is the perfect opportunity to change the undesired characteristics of your heart.

- How grateful are you? What can you point to in your life that reveals a thankful life?

- How do you think others would describe your level of gratefulness? What might this reveal?

- To what extent is unfairness a stumbling block for you? Why?

- Do you tend to focus on what you are *getting* more than on what you are *giving*? What does this tell you?

- List the aspects of your character that are revealed *in conflicts* and the resulting level of *forgiveness* from you (see partial list in *Chapter 6*, last page).

- Which of these character aspects would change if you followed the way of grace and mercy more?

7

THE UNGRATEFUL HEART

Matthew 18:23-35

> *But when that servant went out, he found one of his fellow servants who owed him a hundred denarii. He grabbed him and began to choke him. "Pay back what you owe me!" he demanded.*
>
> verse 28

How quickly he forgot! How easily *we* forget!

Do we really need to remember our ugly sinful past? Sort of, but not exactly; we need to be fully aware that we have been forgiven, despite what we deserve, as well as *how much* we have been forgiven. "But if anyone does not have them [e.g., love, faith, godliness, etc.], he is nearsighted and blind, and has forgotten that he has been cleansed from his past sins" (2 Pet 1:9).

In the midst of the disciples' exciting mountain-top experience, Jesus reminded them where their ultimate joy was to be found:

> The seventy-two returned with joy and said, "Lord, even the demons submit to us in your name." He replied, "I saw Satan fall like lightning from heaven. I have given you authority to trample on snakes and scorpions and to overcome all the power of the enemy; nothing will harm you. *However, do not rejoice that the spirits submit to you, but rejoice that your names are written in heaven.*
>
> Luke 10:17-20, italics added

Our hearts are such that we tend to take the blessings in life for granted (both in the present life and in our life to come). It does not take long before we lose our appreciation for all God has blessed us with. We have an ingrained propensity to focus on the negative at the expense of the positive, on what we *don't* have rather than on all that we do have.

This is at least part of the reason Jesus instituted the Lord's Supper...

We have an ingrained propensity to focus on the negative at the expense of the positive, on what we DON'T have rather than on all that we do have.

"This is my body given for you; do this in remembrance of me." In the same way, after the supper he took the cup, saying, "This cup is the new covenant in my blood, which is poured out for you."

Luke 22:19-20; see also Matt 26:28; 1 Cor 11:23-26

God foreknew our need for and struggle with remembering God's love, mercy, sacrifice, and gift of life. He knew we needed to regularly carry out the Lord's Supper because of our penchant to forget Him. Knowing and appreciating God's love will always lead to a grateful heart. A truly grateful heart will always lead to a forgiving person.

Have you ever given a valuable gift to someone who is not a thankful person? Do you feel like giving this person any more gifts? Is this person generally a happy person? Where is his focus? What does he think he deserves?

All of us need to continually refresh our memory with what God has done for us. We need to dwell on His unmerited gift and love. David expressed this need and desire in the following way: "I remember the days of long ago; I meditate on all your works and consider what your hands have done" (Ps 143:5). The Sons of Korah added, "Within your temple, O God, we meditate on your unfailing love" (Ps 48:9).

Christians have incredible memories…when we *want* them. With the wicked servant, we witness the quintessence of selective memory. This convenient choice of what to remember coincides with our astonishing ability to forget the absolute essentials of life (God, His Word, His love, His forgiveness, and His desires) as well as conveniently overlooking our heinously sinful and selfish nature.

We tend to have total recall over the offenses committed against us. Yet we want our own sins, especially our most embarrassing and atrocious transgressions, to be forgiven and forgotten. While this is understandable, we should never forget who we are, where we came from, Who saved us from all of this, and why (see *Appendix A: Remember To Forget*).

Verse twenty-eight should tell the story of a thoroughly different person. We should be reading about celebrations, shouts of joy, and an astonishing transformation. There should be an Ebenezer Scrooge type elation, delight, compassion, and benevolence after his pardon on Christmas morning.

Nevertheless, after being forgiven an unfathomable amount, a debt he could never come close to paying, and avoiding the harshest of punishments, the servant is seemingly not grateful at all. An ungrateful heart hinders growth and breeds destruction.

Instead of goodwill toward men, the forgiven servant immediately goes out of his way to seek revenge on his fellow servant for a much smaller and insignificant debt. This debt is infinitesimal compared to what the servant was just forgiven. With the monetary terms given, the wicked servant's debt is well over one million to one in ratio to the fellow servant's debt. An ungrateful heart will blind you to reality, love, and God's big picture.

Knowing and appreciating God's love will always lead to a grateful heart.

A truly grateful heart will always lead to a forgiving person.

We should never forget who we are, where we came from, Who saved us from all of this, and why.

An ungrateful heart will blind you to reality, love, and God's big picture.

To illustrate this, let us imagine a man who was pardoned at the very last second from a death sentence being carried out against him. Further, on that very same day, his massive financial debt was forgiven in full *and* he won the lottery in all fifty states. In addition to this, his wife and children were rescued and restored to him after being presumed dead. Later that day, this same man was miraculously cured of several extremely painful and deadly diseases, just in time to receive the news that he had been elected president of the United States. Now, imagine that at the end of this incredible day, this man's first response was to go burn down the house next door because his neighbor had forgotten to return an egg she had borrowed twenty years ago!

What would you say about a person like this? In the words of Nathan the prophet, *you are that person* when you, as a Christian, refuse to forgive!

In the same way, we read that the forgiven servant physically assaulted his fellow servant, demanding "justice" no doubt, immediately after the greatest miracle that could have ever happened to him. The fortunate and blessed servant chose not to be thankful. He failed to grasp, value, and enjoy the most magnificent wonder that anyone in his position could have ever hoped for. As the wicked servant sadly illustrates, God's blessings are the casualties of an ungrateful heart.

How is it even possible to not overflow with joy, gratitude, and generosity after receiving this incredible gift? An ungrateful heart results in the absence of the fruit of the Spirit.

Where was the servant's focus? On God? On fairness? On grace? On the Law? On past offenses/debts? On love? On his "rights"? On himself? Where was his joy? His peace? His hope? His gratitude? His freedom?

Did the forgiven servant believe that he had somehow earned his forgiveness from the master? Did he think that it was his skill and ability to feign contrition that convinced the master of his worthiness? Did he somehow believe the oxymoron that he "deserved mercy" because of his great worth? If so, this would explain why the servant missed out entirely on grace, life, freedom, joy, and love.

Perhaps the wicked and ungrateful servant took on the victim role with regard to his fellow servant? Was he focused on and therefore controlled by the unfairness of the debt he was owed? After being rescued from death through the law and ushered into grace, the servant had "fallen away from grace" (Gal 5:4) and back into the law (fairness, performance, Old Covenant).

Does it not seem completely logical that someone forgiven to that extent would immediately forgive everyone, no matter what the debt? What could possibly prevent this from happening? Perhaps the answer lies in this question: can an ungrateful heart ever truly forgive?

His forgiveness experience should have been the ultimate turning point in his life (as it should be with us). It should have radically changed his heart and way of thinking. God's mercy and grace should have profoundly transformed his view of people, his understanding of life, and his love for God, as well as his treatment of others (2 Cor 5:14-17).

An unchanged person, in the light of such awe-inspiring love and generosity, is both astonishing and dreadful.

What right does the servant have to ask, let alone "demand," anything from anyone ever again? The truly grateful heart willingly and freely forgives all. The grateful heart is free. It is generous. It is humble(d). It is joyful. It knows, experiences, and gives love. It has peace that transcends temporary circumstances. It delights in forgiving. It pleases the Master. It experiences God's intended and promised abundant life. It is a forgiving heart that results in a beautiful life.

Is it safe to say that you are a genuinely grateful person? Is it easy for you to give grace and mercy? Do you still live according to the world's "Fairness Doctrine" or have you "set your hope fully on the grace to be given you when Jesus Christ is revealed" (1 Pet 1:13)? In what specific ways might you need to grow and change?

> For although they knew God, *they neither glorified him as God nor gave thanks to him, but their thinking became futile and their foolish hearts were darkened.*
>
> Romans 1:21, italics added

The truly grateful heart willingly and freely forgives all.

- What are you genuinely thankful for? How often do you sincerely thank God for these things?

- Does your thankfulness tend to revolve around good circumstances? Why?

- How good is your memory? How *selective* is it? Do you have an easier time remembering past hurts or remembering God's loving and gracious gift of salvation? What does this tell you?

- To what extent has God's gift of life transformed your heart? To what extent is it the same?

- How much of a difference is there in your thoughts, motives, desires, behavior, and fruit today than when you were "unforgiven"?

8

OPPORTUNITY LOST

Matthew 18:23-35

His fellow servant fell to his knees and begged him, "Be patient with me, and I will pay you back."

verse 29

His fellow servant responded exactly the same way he did...pleading for mercy. Another prime opportunity presents itself to the forgiven servant. Does he extend the same compassion, love, and forgiveness that he received, or begrudgingly stick to his demands for "fairness"? Imagine the unforgettable impact further mercy would have had on those who saw or heard of his perpetuated grace and mercy.

> *You are the light of the world.* A city on a hill cannot be hidden. Neither do people light a lamp and put it under a bowl. Instead they put it on its stand, and it gives light to everyone in the house. In the same way, *let your light shine before men, that they may see your good deeds and praise your Father in heaven.*
>
> Matthew 5:14-16, italics added

This was a perfect chance to humble himself, put his hope in God, become like Jesus, enjoy the fruit of the Spirit, fulfill God's commands, and store up treasures in heaven. In addition to all of this, he could have avoided the needless heartache that results from refusing to forgive.

Instead of seeing offenses as opportunities, we are inclined to make them into endless possibilities for the flesh. We tend to dwell in self-pity, complain to anyone who will listen (even those who won't), pursue immediate pleasure (hence developing "addictions"), and fantasize about revenge—things which are, in essence, handing over control of our experience to the one who hurt us, conforming to the world, and gratifying our sinful nature, all at the expense of knowing and reliving grace, mercy, and love.

How could the unforgiving servant hear *the same words* that he had cried out to his master and not have been reminded of the mercy that he himself had received? God always has a unique way of evoking the memory of His love and mercy just when we need it most.

How could the unforgiving servant hear the same words that he had cried out to his master and not have been reminded of the mercy that he himself had received?

He divinely, faithfully, and gently refreshes our recollections of His unfailing love and heavenly blessings. It takes a proud, stubborn heart and concerted effort to elude the many reminders and examples of His endless grace.

Jesus knows all too well our propensity to forget, ignore, or blind ourselves to His beauty and love. Yet, He is continually faithful. The reminders are always there if we choose to see them (Ps 19; Rom 1:19-20). His graciousness, love, and mercy should be remembered, meditated upon, and appreciated on a continual basis.

Unforgiveness is a thousand-fold more laborious, draining, and painful to maintain than the most involved forgiveness. Resentment demands a constant flow of your energy to sustain its ugly existence. Bitterness is a deadly parasite that, given enough time, will bleed you dry. In spite of this death and destruction, many Christians unashamedly remain bitter. This merciless and ruthless reaction requires an exceedingly prideful and hard heart.

In what ways does God remind you of His love and gift? How often do you spend significant time just appreciating Jesus and His sacrifice? Where might bitterness have devoured part of your life? Which relationships may have been gunned down by your resentment?

> How often do you spend significant time just appreciating Jesus and His sacrifice?

- What specific reminders of God's love and grace do you see in your life?
  Spend at least five minutes trying to come up with as many reminders of His love as you can and then write them here.

- How much of your life is consumed by remembering/not forgiving the hurts in your life?
  How much time would you save through forgiveness?

- How different would your experience in life be if you occupied your time and thoughts with more of God, His Word, His promises, His blessings, and His gift of salvation?

- What kind of impact does your level of grace or your amount of bitterness have on those around you?

- On a scale of -10 through +10, with -10 being the worst possible bitter and destructive impact, and +10 being the best possible impact of grace, mercy, and love, rate your estimated effect on the following people:

☐	Spouse/Significant Other	☐	Co-Workers
☐	Children	☐	Employees/Boss
☐	Siblings	☐	Fellow Believers
☐	Parents	☐	Non-Believers
☐	Friends	☐	Enemies
☐	Neighbors	☐	Others

We often don't realize the impact we have on others when we make the choice either to walk in grace or refuse to forgive. Whatever you answered, spend time thinking about the influence you've had on the people in your life and where your actions need to change.

- How much were you impacted by one or both of your parents in regard to handling offenses, and the way in which you display either mercy or bitterness?

- What, specifically, would you *change*, if you could, about your parents' level of grace or their level of bitterness, as well as the effect their grace/bitterness had on you? What things about your parents do you wish to *imitate* in this area?

No matter how destructive and painful your upbringing, you do not have to live the same life. You can be an entirely different person, parent, spouse, and friend. This change can take place right now, as you choose to walk in grace and mercy no matter what has happened in the past. Not only *can* this change happen, it *needs* to happen!

9

THE HYPOCRITICAL HEART

Matthew 18:23-35

But he refused. Instead, he went off and had the man thrown into prison until he could pay the debt.

verse 30

Once again, we find the wicked servant aggressively doing the wrong thing. He was demanding and seeking justice for others when he had previously pled for and received mercy for himself. In his mind, he was only doing what was "fair." But his actions and desires were anything but fair against the backdrop of unmerited favor which had been extended to him. This is the height of pride, hypocrisy, stubbornness, and ungratefulness.

The servant seemingly could not shake the idea of receiving what was fair, but only when it favored him. In order to cover his tracks, he probably claimed, as we often do, that he "hated injustice," was merely "protecting his rights," and/or was "only doing what was fair." While there is truth to these statements, they are, in the context of God's unlimited, undeserved love, the deadliest of lies.

Is it wrong for me to give you a thousand dollars, especially when you have done nothing to deserve it? It is horrifically wrong if God wants me to give you a hundred billion dollars. At first glance, a thousand dollar gift may seem like a nice and generous gesture on my part, but in the context of God's grand desire, I fall far short. The reality is, I am greedily withholding from God and others.

This lethal double standard is yet one more way we are like the wicked servant. We have two sets of scales. We want to see justice done when we have been wronged, while thinking little, if any, of mercy. Yet forgiveness, grace, and mercy are all we think about and hope for when we are the one in the wrong. How hypocritical and wicked we are to plead for mercy and yet refuse to give it to others!

Do you see how the passionate pursuit of fairness and our rights must begin to fade as we engage in God's grace? Fairness, while not bad in and of itself, is part of our old way of life. It has now been outmoded and superseded by God's new covenant (i.e., grace). "By calling

> We want to see justice done when we have been wronged, while thinking little, if any, of mercy.
>
> Yet forgiveness, grace, and mercy are all we think about and hope for when we are the one in the wrong.

this covenant 'new,' he has made the first one obsolete; and what is obsolete and aging will soon disappear" (Heb 8:13).

Because "fairness" was still his utmost desire, the servant failed to be changed by God's power and grace (2 Cor 12:9-10). God is not so much in the business of changing circumstances as He is in the business of transforming hearts for His glory (see Jn 11, 15:8). We are easily blinded to God's loving and glorious wish for our ultimate benefit by our narrow-minded passion for happy and just circumstances (see 2 Cor 3:14-18; Heb 12:16-17).

In seeking justice for himself, the servant created a horrific injustice in the eyes of God. This self-serving mission generated trouble and grief for all, especially the Master. Ultimately, however, the hardship would fall completely onto the unforgiving servant (v. 34).

> And *do not grieve the Holy Spirit of God*, with whom you were sealed for the day of redemption. Get rid of all bitterness, rage and anger, brawling and slander, along with every form of malice. Be kind and compassionate to one another, forgiving each other, just as in Christ God forgave you.
>
> Ephesians 4:30-32, italics added

If we choose to live under the idea and desire for fairness as well as all the rules therein, our relationships become more of a *legal obligation* than a *loving relationship*. Our involvement with other people will be based primarily on how well we and they *perform* according to all the unwritten rules and regulations that go into the shifting and biased concept of fairness.

It's no wonder those who live according to the "Fairness Doctrine" are so unhappy. This way of life, like living under the law, only produces more offenses, condemnation, tension, discord, heartache, unfairness, injustice, and conflicts. This was part of God's intent in establishing the law. "The law was added *so that the trespass might increase*" (Rom 5:20a, italics added).

Is this really what you want? Is it wise to place your hope in the idea of fairness? Is this why you are so unhappy? Is this why your relationships are strained? Is this why you feel hopeless? Is this why your experience in life tends to go up or down depending on (controlled by) how others or yourself *perform*? Do you see the connection between this way of life and the bitter life?

But the good news is, if we choose to live under God's grace, even when others offend us, we have an overabundance of the grace and power we need to handle and overcome these expected shortcomings, all for the glory of God. "But where sin increased, *grace increased all the more*" (Rom 5:20b, italics added).

Instead of being bound to and controlled by the sin and weaknesses of others, as well as our own sinful nature, under the New Covenant we have freedom! We are free to forgive. Free to love. Free to encourage. Free to give. Free to grow. Free to enjoy life. Free to enjoy our relationships. Free to bear fruit to God. Free to glorify God.

> So, my brothers, you also died to the law through the body of Christ, that

God is not so much in the business of changing circumstances as He is in the business of transforming hearts for His glory.

In seeking justice for himself, the servant created a horrific injustice in the eyes of God.

If we choose to live under the idea and desire for fairness ... our relationships become more of a legal obligation than a loving relationship.

A Beautiful Life

you might belong to another, to him who was raised from the dead, in order that we might bear fruit to God. For when we were *controlled* by the sinful nature, the sinful passions aroused by the law were at work in our bodies, so that *we bore fruit for death*. But now, by dying to what once bound us, *we have been released from the law so that we serve in the new way of the Spirit, and not in the old way of the written code.*

Romans 7:4-6, italics added

Fairness is great for pointing out problems, but it has few, if any, answers.

Because the wicked servant was enslaved by his focus on himself, his "rights," and living for the illusion of fairness, he was bound to the fruit of the sinful nature (his own and others). What is more, he would eventually miss out on God's intended blessings for his life. Instead of God's desire, he would have a miserable and torturous life. Such is the life of all who lack a heart of mercy and grace when they have received the same.

Fairness is great for pointing out problems, but it has few, if any, answers. In this dark, corrupt, and sinful world we need more answers, not more condemnation. We need hope, power, and help. Jesus did not ignore justice/fairness, but fulfilled it completely (Matt 5:17). He, therefore, is the only answer you will ever need (Jn 14:6, 4:13-14, 6:27, 6:35, 7:37-38, 8:12, 10:9-10, 11:25-26, 15:1-8).

Living for fairness is like living with a harsh and unloving parent. All you are told is, "You never do anything right." There is no encouragement, no optimism, no assistance offered, no hope, no explanations or solutions given. But, you are assured that when you fall short you will be incessantly reminded of your failure (see Matt 5:20, 48).

Living for fairness is like living with a harsh and unloving parent.

When you do achieve what is fair, there is no enjoyment or affirmation. You simply did what was expected. The best case scenario is to achieve a lesser degree of condemnation (note: this way of thinking and the resulting fruit are essentially the same as the perfectionist mindset). Who wants to live with no hope and continual condemnation? Who wouldn't be depressed in this situation? Yet, this is the fruit of the "Fairness Doctrine."

When you refuse to forgive, you reveal where you stand. This pride and stubbornness discloses the location of your hope. You place yourself firmly in the world and its belief in "fairness." As a result, you will reap all the fruit that comes from this decision and misplaced hope (2 Cor 3:6; Gal 6:7-8).

Do you have an over-developed "sense of justice" (in your favor) that drives your thinking, desires, behavior, and level of forgiveness? Have you put all of your hope in the idea of fairness ("eye for eye, and tooth for tooth," the Old Covenant, "under the Law")?

Have you put all of your hope into the idea of fairness?

He forgave us all our sins, *having canceled the written code*, with its regulations, *that was against us and that stood opposed to us*; he took it away, nailing it to the cross. And having disarmed the powers and authorities, he made a public spectacle of them, triumphing over them by the cross.

Colossians 2:13-15, italics added

Fairness "canceled." In a fallen world that is full of sinful people, "the law," the idea of getting what we deserve (i.e., fairness), is not for us but "against us" and stands "opposed to us." Through His forgiveness, His grace, His sacrificial love on the cross, Christ triumphed over the "written code" (Old Covenant) and "its regulations." He supplanted these with a surpassing glory and way of life (New Covenant; see 2 Cor 3:5-18).

Do we really want to go back to the Law, to rules and regulations, to "fairness," to the Old Covenant, to performance, to getting what we deserve, to wrath, to condemnation, to death? Give me grace! Give me freedom! Give me love! Give me peace! Give me hope! Give me abundant life! Give me all that Jesus wants to give me and *not* what I think I deserve or what I truly deserve.

- Do your thoughts, time, and energy go more into changing and/or manipulating circumstances and others, or into God's desire of changing your heart (by responding in ways that trust, love, and glorify God)?

- What does the fruit in your life tell you (e.g., worry, moodiness, anger, joy, peace, continual conflict, etc.)?

- Are your thoughts occupied more by how others are treating you or by concern over how *you* are treating others, in spite of how they might treat you, all to the glory of God? What does this tell you?

- To what extent do you understand and appreciate the New Covenant?

- To what extent do you live like you are free?

- To what extent do you still live like you are under the law?
  (e.g., fairness, controlled by performance, demanding your "rights", resentment)

- What do your *relationships* reveal concerning your allegiance to either fairness or grace?

10

When the other servants saw what had happened, they were greatly distressed and went and told their master everything that had happened.

verse 31

"See to it that no one misses the grace of God and that no bitter root grows up to cause trouble and defile many" (Heb 12:15).

Ungratefulness is a repulsive stench. Unforgiveness grieves all who witness it (Hebrews 12:15). Most importantly, it grieves God (Eph 4:30-32). No one wins and *everyone loses with unforgiveness*—except the enemy. Satan's passionate desire to "divide and conquer" rules the day when we do not forgive. We become co-conspirators of the devil's perpetual plot to rob, kill, and destroy whenever we reject God's desire for mercy and grace.

This is precisely why marriages struggle and fail. Husbands and wives constantly fight each other (thus dividing the union between each other and God), instead of combating the problem, their own selfish desires, and the enemy. Of course they will be miserable. Of course they will fail. Marriage, above all other relationships, should overflow with grace, compassion, mercy, and love.

On the flip side, *everyone wins* and only Satan loses when we forgive. You can never go wrong with grace and mercy. Our contemptible enemy is always crushed and defeated when we reflect God's glory by imitating His gracious pardon of our countless offenses. Forgiveness is always a win, win, win situation!

So many families shattered, marriages ruined, friendships destroyed, brother and sister relationships broken—all from the stubborn, prideful, ungrateful refusal to live in grace and mercy. Are your "rights" really worth this trouble and anguish? Is holding onto and reliving past hurts worth the present and future destruction in your life and relationships? Who comes out on top through your stubbornness? (Hint: *NOT YOU!*)

No one wins and everyone loses with unforgiveness— except the enemy.

On the flip side, everyone wins and only Satan loses when we forgive.

Do you ever refuse genuine love? Why then do you refuse to give this same love? Did you refuse God's grace? Then why would you refuse to give the same?

Instead of picking sides and becoming combatants in this escalating conflict, the other servants took appropriate action (see preceding verses, Matt 18:15-20, in how to handle conflict). Injustice should motivate us to do what is right (not necessarily what is fair) out of a desire to love God and others. Practically speaking, we can help others by helping them work on the problems (not adding to them!). This can be achieved only by going to the Master *first* (see Jas 4:1-3; Matt 6:33; 2 Chr 18:4; 1 Sam 23:2-9).

In the midst of a conflict, many Christians tend to: judge (Jas 4:11-12) who is wrong (often after listening to only one side; Prov 18:17), enlist our allegiance to the (perceived) victimized side (Prov 28:21), and recruit more warriors by gossiping to others (Prov 26:20), all in our emotional and fleshly attempt to "help" resolve the clash of sinners and cymbals (1 Cor 13:1).

We typically feed the fire of discord (Prov 26:20), however well-intentioned, while neglecting to bring hope, truth, responsibility, and love to the dire situation. It is not our job to solve the problem or to make anyone feel better (e.g., by letting them "vent;" Prov 29:11). We need to speak the truth in love (Eph 4:15; 1 Cor 13:6; Matt 18:15; Prov 10:11, 31-32), tell them not what they *want* to hear (Prov 26:28; Ps 12:2-3; Jer 6:14), but what they *need* to hear (Prov 27:5-6, 28:23; Eph 4:29), in the hope that faithfulness to God and His design (Matt 18:15-20; Lk 17:3; Gal 6:1) will lead to repentance for all involved (2 Tim 2:25-26; Rom 2:4).

How much hope, love, and truth do you bring to your conflicts? How about the conflicts of others? Can you easily say that you glorify God in the conflicts that you are a part of? Do others know, beyond a shadow of a doubt, they are loved by you in the midst of your conflicts, even if and especially when you do not resolve the situation? How often do you go to God with the right motives (Jas 4:1-3) and tell Him "everything" (i.e., not conveniently leaving out your responsibilities) while in the midst of a conflict?

> Injustice should motivate us to do what is right (not necessarily what is fair).

> How much hope, love, and truth do you bring to your conflicts?

- How often have you truly followed the steps in Matthew 18:15-20?
  How often have you refused or failed to follow God's design for conflict? Why do you think that is?

- Who typically comes out the "loser" in your conflicts (e.g., Satan, God, you, others)? Why?

- Is holding onto and re-living past hurts worth the present and future destruction in your life and relationships? Why or why not?

- How often do you see other people as the enemy rather than pouring your time and effort into the actual problems?

- Which of your relationships might have been damaged or destroyed through *your* stubbornness and pride?

- Do you tend to "speak the truth," but not really in a loving way?
  Or, do you try to avoid the full truth so as to spare the feelings of others? Why? How helpful is this approach?

- How often do you actually "speak the truth in love" (Eph. 4:15, 29; I Cor. 13:6)?
  What might lead up to your decision not to speak the truth in a loving way?

11

THE SELFISH HEART

Matthew 18:23-35

Then the master called the servant in. "You wicked servant," he said, "I canceled all that debt of yours because you begged me to."

verse 32

The Master precisely describes not just the servant's behavior, but who he really is—wicked! His actions reveal his heart (Jer 17:9; Mk 7:21-23; Gen 6:5; Deut 8:2, Lk 8:13). Most likely the servant was sorry only because he had been caught, rather than being truly grieved over his repulsive behavior and treatment of his master. To some, this difference may seem trivial, but to God, *your motive means everything* (1 Sam 16:7; 1 Chr 29:17; 2 Chr 6:20, 16:9; Prov 16:2). In addition, your motivation has a direct bearing on the degree of actual change in your heart.

Jesus emphasized the motives in our hearts when He said, "The good man brings good things out of the good stored up in his heart, and the evil man brings evil things out of the evil stored up in his heart" (Lk 6:45). What was in the servant's heart? What is in your heart?

In one sense, God does not really care about your outward appearance and performance. For Him, it is always a matter of your heart. Jesus consistently delivered harsh condemnation to the Pharisees and teachers of the law even though their behavior was superior. Why? Because He knew their hearts. "These people honor me with their lips, but their hearts are far from me" (Matt 15:8).

Your motivation is especially significant when it comes to forgiveness, change, and salvation. Paul identifies two distinct motives that could not be further apart, both in purity and outcome:

> *Godly sorrow* brings *repentance* that leads to *salvation* and leaves *no regret*, but *worldly sorrow* brings *death*. See what this godly sorrow has *produced in you*: what earnestness, what eagerness to clear yourselves, what

> To God, your motive means EVERYTHING.

> "The Lord does not look at the things man looks at. Man looks at the outward appearance, but the Lord looks at the heart."
>
> 1 Samuel 16:7

indignation, what alarm, what longing, what concern, what readiness to see justice done.

2 Corinthians 7:10-11, italics added

Do you see the extreme contrast in fruit? Godly sorrow is immensely rewarding and enormously fruitful. The many signs of godly motivation are unmistakable: life, love, joy, boldness, forgiveness, peace, deliverance, loving relationships, changed hearts, and glory to God. On the other hand, the *only thing* that worldly motivation has to offer is *death*!

This immeasurable contrast is due simply to a difference in motives. Your motivation essentially depends on what is in your heart (Prov 4:23; Rom 8:5-8; Col 3:1-2). In one way, your heart is the combination of your desires and beliefs. These reflect what is important to you (e.g., truth, respect, happiness, love, hard work, pleasure, money, God, feeling good, holiness, self, others, etc.).

FEAR OF MAN:

The craving for people to think highly of you.

For example, if you have a strong desire for people to think highly of you, then what you say and do will be motivated, influenced, and even controlled by what the Bible calls "the fear of man" (Prov 29:25). You will attempt to please people (manipulation) in the hope that they will bring pleasure to you. "Everything they do is done for men to see" (Matt 23:5).

In contrast, if you value pleasing God (i.e., love), then your thoughts and actions will reveal what the Bible calls "the fear of God" (Ps 19:9; Prov 14:27; 15:33; 16:6; Ecc 12:13). You will strive to please God no matter what others think or what happens to your temporary circumstances (Gal 1:10; Phil 4:11-12; 1 Thes 4:1). *"We are not trying to please men but God, who tests our hearts"* (1 Thes 2:4, italics added).

FEAR OF GOD:

The passion to please God no matter what others think or what happens to your temporary circumstances.

Jesus summed up the motivation of our hearts like only Jesus can when He said:

> *Do not store up for yourselves treasures on earth,* where moth and rust destroy, and where thieves break in and steal. *But store up for yourselves treasures in heaven,* where moth and rust do not destroy, and where thieves do not break in and steal. *For where your treasure is, there your heart will be also.*

Matthew 6:19-21, italics added

When what you hold dear (i.e., "your treasure") is denied or violated, then you become angry and/or grieved. If *you* are what is most important, then your motivation and actions will tend to be directed toward pleasing your self (self-love, self-importance, self-centered). The more important *God* is to you, the more your desire and behavior will be focused on loving and pleasing God (Heb 11:6; 2 Cor 5:9; Eph 4:30; Matt 6:33; Col 1:10).

When what you hold dear (i.e., "your treasure") is denied or violated, then you become angry and/or grieved.

Godly sorrow comes from godly love. Worldly sorrow comes from worldly "love," which is *self-love*—i.e., love for the world and the things of the world; self-importance; self-seeking; self-gratification; selfishness; lack of love or concern for God, His Word, and His design; and lack of love or concern for others (see Rom 2:8; 1 Cor 13:1-8; 2 Cor 5:15; Phil 3:6-9; 2 Tim 3:1-8, 4:3-4, 9; Jas 3:13-4:4).

Godly sorrow is being grieved, angry, even broken over the things that bring sorrow to God and separate you from Him. What is precious to God is precious to you. This can come only from love for God. When a person experiences true godly sorrow, he is *highly motivated* to please God (2 Cor 5:9; Gal 5:6; Eph 4:29-32, 5:10; Heb 11:6) and glorify Him (1 Cor 10:31; Col 3:17).

This kind of motivation (love) usually leads to repentance (change) on our part (2 Cor 7:10-11; Matt 7:5). Godly sorrow/love for God also causes us to hate whatever God hates—e.g., falsehood, evil, injustice, etc. (see Rom 12:9; Ps 36:1-4, 119:104, 119:127-128, 119:163; Prov 8:13; Amos 5:15).

Paul exalted and maximized God's purpose and motivation of love when he wrote to the church in Galatia: "The *only thing* that counts is *faith* expressing itself through *love*" (Gal 5:6, italics added). Absolutely nothing you do in life "counts" unless it is done "through love." This makes perfect sense, especially to God who "is love." This also fits precisely into the universal desire for love (although much of this is twisted and perverted by the world and our sinful natures).

What is the real cause for failing to meet our desired goals? Why are we unable to achieve true and lasting forgiveness? The primary reason is our selfish, loveless, and impure *motives* (2 Tim 3:1-8; Mk 7:6-13; Lk 11:43-44; 1 Tim 6:9-10). What we cherish is not in line with God's desires. James admonishes us by writing, "When you ask, you do not receive, because you ask with *wrong motives*, that you may spend what you get on *your pleasures*" (Jas 4:3, italics added).

Paul emphasized the right kind of motive for any and all goals we may have: "The goal of this command is *love*, which comes from a *pure heart* and a *good conscience* and a *sincere faith*" (1 Tim 1:5, italics added). Love is valuing God and others above ourselves (see 2 Cor 5:15; Jn 15:13; 1 Jn 3:16; Phil 2:3-8).

Without love, we are rejecting God's purpose and way of life while aligning our desires, thinking, and pursuits with what the world treasures (cp. Rom 12:2). The world does not know love or God (1 Cor 1:18, 2:14; 1 Jn 2:11, 3:10, 3:14, 4:8). In fact, it *hates* God and all that He is about (Jn 3:19-20). Underlining this fact, James writes: "You adulterous people, don't you know that friendship with the world is hatred toward God? Anyone who chooses to be a friend of the world becomes an enemy of God" (Jas 4:4).

However, whenever we truly love (i.e., "with actions and in truth; see 1 Jn 3:17-18, 4:16-18; Jas 2:15-17), no matter what the situation, no matter how others react, no matter what happens in the end, *we have achieved one hundred percent success!* We have loved! We have been faithful to God's heart. We have put our hope in Him. Therefore we have pleased, imitated, loved, and glorified God. This is all we can do. "Love never fails" (1 Cor 13:8).

Love is all we are called to do. *Attempting anything in addition to love is not love.* With this type of fleshly effort, we cross the line into the realm of God's responsibilities, as well as the responsibility of others. Not only is this sin, it is unprofitable at best, and usually destructive to all involved.

Absolutely nothing you do in life "counts" unless it is done "through love."

Without love we are rejecting God's purpose and way of life.

Whenever we truly love, no matter what the situation, no matter how others react, no matter what happens in the end, we have achieved one hundred percent success!

Unfortunately, we often gauge success by the response of others, their treatment of us, and/or our ability to change the situation. The reality is that we have very little, if anything, to do with the change that happens outside of us. That is the Holy Spirit's job. The only impact we can hope to have is if we are faithful to God's desire and design (i.e., His love and His Word).

Your job is not to change others, it is to love them. Yet we usually get this backwards. This reversal of God's intention is the main reason why we are unhappy, struggling, and failing in relationships.

If you faithfully love another person, especially in confrontations, conflicts, and arguments, then you have accomplished precisely what God desires of you—no more, no less—no matter the outcome. When we truly love, we put our hope in God (see 1 Pet 3:1-12; 1 Tim 4:9-12, 6:17; Ps 42) and His timing, wisdom, love, and power to bring about *His* desired results when *He* deems best.

> Those who oppose him he must gently instruct, *in the hope that God will* grant them repentance leading them to a knowledge of the truth.
>
> 2 Timothy 2:25, italics added

When I lack in, or fail to, love, not only am I sinning, but I am attempting to achieve what is impossible. The reality is that I am trying to change or manipulate a person or situation so that I will be happy. What is worse, I am trying to take the place of God! I am living outside of truth and within a lie. Therefore, I will always, always, always fail miserably, even if I am sometimes temporarily gratified (i.e., through manipulation, intimidation, sarcastic insults, criticizing, etc.).

The inevitable experience derived from playing God is worry, anger, frustration, and fighting that ultimately leads to bitterness, despair, depression, and destruction. If you tend to experience these things, then look for the ways in which you may lack love, attempt to play God, and put your hope in yourself, others, and circumstances.

While a change in circumstances or another person is *a* goal, it is not *the* goal. A teacher teaches, an evangelist preaches, a counselor counsels, a parent trains, all for a much desired change from individuals in their audiences. But the actual change, the responses and decisions made by the individuals are out of their hands. Yet, by loving them with the truth of God's Word, they have afforded a wealth of hope for the desired transformation to occur.

The ugly reality is that if our motivation is not love, if we do something for any reason outside of love, even if the whole world applauds, *it is hideous to God* (i.e., sinful; see Matt 6). In conflict and difficulties especially, in the heat of battle, we tend to take matters into our own hands, all at the expense of love and faithfulness.

> *Let love and faithfulness never leave you;*
> Bind them around your neck,
> write them on the tablet of your heart.

Your job
Is not to
change others,
it is to love
them.

When I lack in,
or fail to, love,
not only am I
sinning, but I am
attempting to
achieve what is
impossible.

While a
change in
circumstances or
another person is
A goal, it is not
THE goal.

Then you will win favor and a good name
in the sight of God and man.

Proverbs 3:3-4, italics added

The assumed and unfortunate prime directive of many husbands and wives is the transformation of their spouses. This goal may start off with good intentions, but it quickly disintegrates into nagging, fighting, screaming, self-pity, "the silent treatment," manipulation, pouting, anger, etc. Again, transformation is God's task, combined with our spouse's responsibility. My job is not to change my "better half," *it is to love them* (Eph 5:22-33; Col 3:17-19; Jn 15:12-13).

God is not going to ask you, "How much did you change your wife?" or "What is your success-to-failure ratio in solving conflicts?" or "How well did you succeed in getting your husband to fulfill you and meet all your needs?" He is interested in how faithful you are to His passion and purpose. You will probably hear something like, "How much did you love those I put in your life, especially the difficult people in difficult circumstances?" (Matt 5:38-48) "More importantly, how much did you love your spouse and family?" (Eph 5:22-33; 1 Tim 5:4, 8) We are simply called to be good stewards of the people and love He gave us (Matt 25:14-30; Rom 5:5). On that final day, when standing before God, how confident will you be of your stewardship of His love and calling?

> God is love. Whoever lives in love lives in God, and God in him. In this way, love is made complete among us so that we will have confidence on the day of judgment, because in this world we are like him.

1 John 4:16b-17

What is *the* greatest command? What is at the top of God's list for us to do? What is of utmost importance to Him, who is supreme? It is *not* getting our way, winning fights, achieving happiness and fulfillment, or even resolving conflict. It is love! (Mk 12:30-31; Jn 13:34-35; Gal 5:6; 1 Jn; 2 Jn 5-6)

His desire is that we know Him and His love so that we will love God, as well as love everyone else (Eph 5:1-3; 1 Jn 4:16-17; 2 Jn 5-6). If love is so essential, if it is God's premier purpose and defining characteristic, then you need to consider your life *without* love:

- Without love **all that I do is sin**   (Mk 12:30-31)

- Without love **"I am nothing"**   (1 Cor 13:2)

- Without love **"I gain nothing"**   (1 Cor 13:3)

- Without love **I can do nothing**   (Jn 15:5; 2 Pet 1:3-4)

- Without love **I remain in darkness**   (1 Jn 2:11)

- Without love **I am not a child of God**   (1 Jn 3:10)

Sidebar:

What is
the greatest
command?

What is
at the top
of God's list
for us to do?

It is not
getting our way,
winning fights,
achieving happiness
and fulfillment, or
even resolving
conflict.

It is LOVE!

- Without love **I cannot know God** (1 Jn 4:8)

- Without love **I am full of fear** (1 Jn 4:18)

- Without love **nothing I do counts** (Gal 5:6)

- Without love **I remain in death** (1 Jn 3:14)

How well do you know God and His love? How much does God's love drive your thoughts and actions? To what extent do you "live in love"? (1 Jn 4:16) How much do others see God's love in you? What does the fruit in your life and relationships reveal?

Always check your motivation. "Examine yourselves to see whether you are in the faith; test yourselves" (2 Cor 13:5). Know *why* and for *whom* you are doing what it is you want to do. "Love must be sincere. Hate what is evil; cling to what is good. Be devoted to one another in brotherly love. Honor one another above yourselves" (Rom 12:9-10). The motivation of your heart can be the difference between life and death! So follow Solomon's wisdom, "*Above all else*, guard your heart, for it is the wellspring of life" (Prov 4:23, italics added).

We, like Solomon's father, King David, "the man after God's own heart," (1 Sam 13:14) should request the following of God:

> *Test me*, O Lord, and try me,
> *examine my heart and my mind*;
> for your love is ever before me,
> and I walk continually in your truth.
>
> Psalm 26:2, italics added

> *Search me*, O God, and know my heart;
> *test me* and know my anxious thoughts.
> See if there is any offensive way in me,
> and lead me in the way everlasting.
>
> Psalm 139:23-24, italics added

> May the words of my mouth and
> the meditation of my heart
> be pleasing in your sight,
> O Lord, my Rock and my Redeemer.
>
> Psalm 19:14

Where do we get the proper motivation? What is the only source of true love? Who do we tend to forsake? (Jer 2:13, 19)

"Let us love one another, for *love comes from God*" (1 Jn 4:7, italics added). "This is love: *not that we loved God, but that he loved us* and sent his Son as an atoning sacrifice for our sins"

The motivation of your heart can be the difference between life and death.

"May the words of my mouth and the meditation of my heart be pleasing in your sight, O Lord."

Psalm 19:4

A Beautiful Life

(1 Jn 4:10, italics added). "God is love. And so we know and rely on the love God has for us" (1 Jn 4:16). "*We love because he first loved us*" (1 Jn 4:19, italics added).

God's love is the only thing that will bring about lasting change in our own hearts, true forgiveness of others, and glory to Him. Praise God that He has so fully and abundantly blessed us with His love.

> And hope does not disappoint us, because *God has poured out his love into our hearts* by the Holy Spirit, whom he has given us.
>
> Romans 5:5, italics added

(See also Ps 23:5-6, 26:3, 32:10, 33:5, 33:18, 33:22, 34:9-10, 36:5; Eph 3:16-20; Col 2:10; 1 Pet 1:3-4.)

In light of the magnitude and significance of God's love and mercy, what a wicked thing it is when we refuse to forgive *anyone* for *anything*. As Christians, we have pleaded for, and been granted unlimited mercy and grace. Therefore, rejecting God's desire to forgive reveals self-importance/self-love rather than a heart that treasures God and His desires.

Once you beg for and receive mercy, you can never go back. You cannot ask for and enter the New Covenant (grace, love, freedom, life) and then, whenever you think it is convenient for you, go back to the Old Covenant (the Law, condemnation, fairness). You have forfeited any and all rights to hold *anything* against *anyone ever* again! "You are not under law, but under grace" (Rom 6:14).

Imagine going next door and informing your neighbor that his house now belongs to you. What is your reasoning? What right do you have to make such a claim? Informing your neighbor that you simply want his property is not going to cut it. However laughable and absurd such an endeavor would be, it is precisely the same when it comes to Christians and forgiveness. We have exactly the same right to hold something against another as we have to demand our neighbor's house.

Instead of being motivated to seek first *my* kingdom, while protecting my rights and "saving my life," I need to seek *first* God's kingdom while taking advantage of the *opportunities* to pick up my cross and lose my life. One quick glance at your life will reveal that these opportunities abound.

Remember, just as this servant, we too are going to be called before the Master. It is not simply *what* you do that matters; rather, it is infinitely more important *why* you do what you do. If you are brutally honest with yourself, what do you think God will say to you, particularly concerning His love, grace, and mercy given or withheld by you? Have you been faithful with what has been entrusted to you? Or might you hear something along the lines of, "You wicked servant"?

As you can clearly see, your motive is what separates the men from the boys, so to speak. It is the difference between "hay and straw," or "gold, silver, and costly stones."

God's love is the only thing that will bring about lasting change in our own hearts, true forgiveness of others, and glory to Him.

Once you beg for and receive mercy, you can never go back. You cannot enter the New Covenant and then, whenever you think it is convenient for you, go back to the Old Covenant.

For no one can lay any foundation other than the one already laid, which is Jesus Christ. If any man builds on this foundation using gold, silver, costly stones, wood, hay or straw, *his work will be shown for what it is, because the Day will bring it to light*. It will be revealed with fire, and *the fire will test the quality of each man's work*. If what he has built survives, he will receive his reward. If it is burned up, he will suffer loss; he himself will be saved, but only as one escaping through the flames.

1 Corinthians 3:11-15, italics added

Your foundation, your treasure, the true motive in your heart, the measure of love you have for God and others "will be revealed with fire." "The day will bring it to light." Will you "suffer loss," or will you enjoy both temporary and eternal rewards?

If you say, "But we knew nothing about this," *does not he who weighs the heart perceive it*? Does not he who guards your life know it? Will he not repay each person according to what he has done?

Proverbs 24:12, italics added

For God will bring every deed into judgment, *including every hidden thing,* whether it is good or evil.

Ecclesiastes 12:14, italics added

There is nothing concealed that will not be disclosed, or hidden that will not be made known. What you have said in the dark will be heard in the daylight, and what you have whispered in the ear in the inner rooms will be proclaimed from the roofs.

Luke 12:2-3, italics added

Therefore judge nothing before the appointed time; wait till the Lord comes. *He will bring to light what is hidden in darkness and will expose the motives of men's hearts.* At that time each will receive his praise from God.

1 Corinthians 4:5, italics added

For the word of God...judges the thoughts and attitudes of the heart. Nothing in all creation is hidden from God's sight. *Everything is uncovered and laid bare before the eyes of him to whom we must give account.*

Hebrews 4:12-13, italics added

Blessed are the *merciful,* For they will be shown mercy.
Blessed are the *pure in heart*, for they will see God.
Blessed are the peacemakers, for they will be called sons of God.

Matthew 5:7-9, italics added

It is not simply WHAT you do that matters; rather, it is infinitely more important WHY you do what you do.

Have you been faithful with what has been entrusted to you?

"Does not he who weighs the heart perceive it?"

Proverbs 24:12

A Beautiful Life

- In light of all of the scriptures which describe your absolute need to love others, where do you see room for growth in your own life?

- What is of utmost importance to you? Where is your treasure?
  When you encounter offenses, what is revealed concerning what you truly value?

- What is revealed by your thoughts and behavior regarding what is most important to you?

- List every right you have to hold a sin against another.

- How often do you look for, find, and act upon opportunities to lose your life?

- Approximately what percentage of these opportunities do you pass up (50%, 99%)? What might this reveal about your heart/motives/love?

- What is the typical resulting fruit in your life from this action or inaction (e.g., fruit of the Spirit, growth, stagnation, love, anger, reconciliation, bitterness)?

- Would your family, friends, and co-workers easily characterize you as "merciful" (i.e., full of mercy)? Why or why not?

- To what extent is love (for God and others) your *primary* motivating factor? How often are you driven by selfish reasons?

- How often do you argue, fight, and attempt to resolve conflict *without love*? How successful are you when you do attempt this?

12

IMITATORS OF CHRIST?

Matthew 18:23-35

"Shouldn't you have had mercy on your fellow servant just as I had on you?"

Verse 33

"Be imitators of God, therefore, as dearly loved children and *live a life of love, just as Christ loved us and gave himself up for us* as a fragrant offering and sacrifice to God" (Eph 5:1-2, italics added).

The goal, God's call, His desire and command is that, "as dearly loved children," you *imitate* Jesus, by living "*a life of love.*" We are to have the *same* grace, mercy, forgiveness, and love toward others just as Christ had toward us. "Be kind and compassionate to one another, *forgiving each other, just as in Christ God forgave you*" (Eph 4:32, italics added).

God wants you to see others through the eyes of compassion and grace (just as *you* want to be understood) rather than performance, demands, expectations, "needs," guilt, "my fair share," and condemnation. You will find it infinitely easier to live and forgive when you follow God's desire and design.

"But what about my rights?" By issue of our faith and God's forgiveness, our rights belong to Jesus. We need to purposefully entrust these, along with everything else, to God out of faith in, and love for, Jesus.

> That is why I am suffering as I am. Yet I am not ashamed, because I know whom I have believed, and am convinced that he is able to guard what I have *entrusted* to him for that day.
>
> 2 Timothy 1:12, italics added

We should no longer, as followers and imitators of Christ, follow and imitate the world by living for our rights (Matt 5:38-47; Lk 9:23-24; Gal 2:20; Phil 3:7-11). Instead we live to trust, please, honor, love, and glorify God. Our "rights" are mere stumbling blocks to God's will for us.

By issue of our faith and God's forgiveness, our rights belong to Jesus.

Therefore, I urge you, brothers, *in view of God's mercy*, to offer your bodies as *living sacrifices*, holy and pleasing to God--this is your spiritual act of worship. Do not conform any longer to the pattern of this world, but be transformed by the renewing of your mind. Then you will be able to test and approve what God's will is—his good, pleasing and perfect will.

Romans 12:1-2, italics added

Our "rights" are mere stumbling blocks to God's will for us.

How many rights does a willing and living sacrifice have? We are called, "in view of God's mercy," not to live for our rights, but to surrender our rights for His glory. We are called to please God, not ourselves. We are called to conform to God's desire and design, not the world's. God's character and activity in our lives should lead to worship of the only One who is worthy of praise, love, and adoration.

What are your rights? Which rights do you tend to live for (and die for!)? What are the things in your life that become stumbling blocks to God's will for you? What specific "rights" (desires) have you not entrusted over to God?

- Which aspects of your imitation of Jesus do you need to work on
  (e.g., love, grace, forgiveness, kindness, patience, self-control, compassion, humility, pure motives, lack of concern for self)?

- To whom do your rights belong? Why?

- What does your level of anger and resentment reveal concerning who you perceive to be the true owner of your rights?

- Can you identify the specific "stumbling blocks" (rights) in your life?

- In what ways do you seek to find your life here on earth?

13

THE UGLY LIFE

Matthew 18:23-35

In anger his master turned him over to the jailers to be tortured, until he should pay back all he owed.

verse 34

The ugly consequences of unforgiveness are prison and torture! When we choose to not forgive others (in the same way that we were graciously and totally forgiven by God) *we* indict, convict, and condemn *ourselves*. No judge or jury is needed. We are given the most extreme consequence, by ourselves, for *our* heinous crime. We are thrown into a deep and dark dungeon (i.e., we *willingly* give up our freedom) by our own hand. In one way, we give control of our life's experience to the very person who hurt us!

As if this punishment was not enough, we repeatedly submit ourselves to torture! We continuously relive the pain of the offense over and over and over... What is more, we *voluntarily* and *willfully* remain in this tortuous existence indefinitely.

Suppose someone inflicted a serious wound to your body. With the damage already done, the wise thing to do would be to take care of the injury by whatever means necessary. But, what if, instead of cleaning and dressing the wound and giving it time to heal, you decided to periodically stab it with a knife? With each plunge beneath your skin, you experience searing pain. What is more, every day you continually jab, prod, cut, and stab the same deep cut. Will it ever heal? Or will your daily experience be filled with piercing and throbbing pain? This is the ugly and undeniable experience of the unforgiving person.

This explains all of the misery (e.g., depression, destruction, worry, paranoia, addictions, fear, despair, loneliness, bizarre behavior, critical heart, etc.) that accompanies our refusal to forgive others. Feeling the offense and hurt continually is a perfect example of torture.

It is not always the level of impact or pain, but the *repetition* of that pain that will bring about the most vile and miserable torture! An apt illustration of this is the infamous Chinese Water Torture. It consists solely of one drop of water, *repeatedly* dripped on one's forehead. What at first glance might seem harmless, when given enough time and repetition, becomes a highly effective method of torture. In just the same way, even

> When we refuse to forgive, we give control of our life's experience to the very person who hurt us.

the smallest offense, relived over and over, results in excruciating torment for the unforgiving soul.

Forgiveness, as with all of God's commands, is for our benefit and freedom. The call to freely forgive is just another wonderful reflection of His loving character, not an unjust and unreasonable demand.

In addition to choosing his own torture, the wicked servant angered the master. The *last* thing a believer should want to do is to make God angry. What a dreadful position to be in! (Jer 2:19; Matt 7:21-23, 25:26-30; Heb 10:29-31; Rev 20:10, 15) While God is love, He is still a God of justice, and there are always consequences to our folly and sin.

Yet many times we lack true concern for our sin, as well as grief over how that sin grieves God. The right and pure motivation (i.e., "godly sorrow," love for God, fear of God) is absolutely essential for changing our hearts, changing our behavior, and effecting true forgiveness.

The tragic irony, for the unforgiving servant, is that he ultimately did receive justice. He turned his back to grace, hoping to recover something from his past. In turn, the master gives him what he deserves—prison and torture—instead of mercy and grace (see Heb 10:29).

> The LORD preserves the faithful,
> but the proud he pays back in full.
>
> Psalm 31:23

Be careful what you ask for. Be even more careful what you *demand*!

> **The tragic irony, for the unforgiving servant, is that he ultimately did receive justice.**

- Have you ever experienced the imprisonment and torture of unforgiveness? If yes, for how long and how often?

- What set you free? Or are you still a prisoner, continuing to experience torture?

- What are you doing or not doing that angers God?
  Do you think that your level of grace and mercy pleases God or grieves and angers Him? Why?

- What changes are you going to implement in order to grieve or anger God less?

- Who do you know that is living a tortuous life due to his or her resentment? List their names here and begin to pray for them. Pray also for ways in which you can share the freeing and life-changing principles of love, grace, and mercy with them.

14

IT'S ALWAYS A MATTER OF THE HEART

Matthew 18:23-35

This is how my Heavenly Father will treat each of you unless you forgive your brother from your heart.

verse 35

Jesus warns us that we will experience God's wrath in the same way as the wicked servant unless we forgive others *from our heart* (that is, a heart that knows and values grace, and, therefore, can *freely* grant forgiveness). "I desire *mercy*, not sacrifice" (Hos 6:6, italics added; see also Matt 9:13, 12:7).

If you are being tortured by your stubborn and prideful decisions, there is still hope. However, that hope comes at the expense of your stubbornness and pride. You hold the keys to your freedom as well as to the end of your *self-imposed* anguish. The choice is still the same…to forgive or not to forgive. It is up to you to forgive completely, just as Christ forgave you.

> Blessed are the merciful, for they will be shown mercy.
>
> Matthew 5:7

Here is the key to forgiveness, and it cannot be emphasized enough: *your heart needs to change.* And not just any change will do. You need to experience, know, and cherish God's unfailing love, unlimited mercy, and His boundless grace. In so doing, your heart will be more like His. Grace, mercy, and love are the key ingredients that transform the heart of any person. In knowing God, you will know these things.

Forgiveness is not just something that you do; it must flow from a heart that has been transformed by God's loving kindness. A heart that desires to please God will desire to forgive. A heart that deeply loves God is at ease in pardoning others. The heart that longs to glorify God will aspire to emulate Christ at the peak of His glory…His unfathomable act of sacrificial love that afforded forgiveness for all.

As we have seen, over and over, the more you know and treasure God's love, the more your heart will become like His, and the less effort it will take for you to forgive. However, the

You hold the keys to your freedom.

A heart that desires to please God will desire to forgive.

opposite is also true. Lacking in knowledge and appreciation of who God is, all that He graciously bestows, and what He desires, reveals an *unyielding heart* and the root of your struggle to forgive.

In addition to all of this, it is highly advantageous to understand, trust, and appreciate the *sovereignty of God* in regard to your suffering (see Job, Joseph, Jeremiah, Jesus, Paul, etc.). God, in all of His *wisdom, love, power,* and *goodness,* has allowed *every* last painful experience in your life (Lam 3:32-38).

We need to be conscious of the fact that God is always working on more than we can see or grasp, especially in the bad times. God often sacrifices our temporary happiness for the greater and lasting good—e.g., His kingdom, our faith, our righteousness, our character, His glory, our relationship with Him, etc. (see John 11; Rom 5:1-5; 2 Cor 1:8-9, 4:16-18, 12:9-10; Heb 11; 1 Pet 1:6-9). Without this understanding, we will not appreciate affliction.

Understanding pain and suffering requires the utmost trust in *God's character.* We need to entrust our experiences to our infinite, eternal, all-powerful, all-loving, just, holy, and *perfect* God, whose ways are infinitely higher than ours (Is 55:8-9). Without faith in God's character, we will be unable to understand, appreciate, benefit from, or truly forgive the offenses in our lives (see Rom 8:28-39; Heb 11).

The people who bring and/or have brought you pain are used by God, in His wisdom, love, sovereignty, and plan, to work out *in you,* through the process of sanctification, His desired change in your heart and life (Rom 8:28-29; 1 Thes 4:3; Jas 1:2-4; Gen 50:20). God, in His love for you, values your conformity to His image, your growth in Him, the fruit you produce, and your holiness (Heb 12:5-11; Jn 15:1-17) immeasurably more than your temporary pleasure, comfort, and happiness. Because this is God's grand desire, it should be yours too! "*Your* kingdom come, *your* will be done" (Matt 6:10, italics added).

In one way, the offending people in your life are always one hundred percent responsible for their actions; but it will make your life easier to see that they are mere unwitting agents of change in your life (potentially). In addition, you need to understand that their offenses are used for the glory of God (Gen 50:20; 1 Pet 1:7), just like *your* sin is used in the lives of others, and for God's glory. However, it is one thing to recognize the role people play in God's plan for you, but it is quite another to respond in God's ideal way (i.e., with love, grace, and mercy).

The betrayal, the treachery, the selfishness, the harshness of others are often the driving forces that bring about the much needed change that we ourselves desire (if not at that moment, later in life; see Ps 51; Heb 12:5-11) and need. It is not so much what others might do to us that matters, but it is *how* and *why* we respond (Matt 5:38-48). Do we allow it/them to impede and control our lives, or are we motivated by love (and the pain) to move closer to God, to trust Him, to conform to His Son, to lose our life, to put our hope outside of this world, to love others, and to glorify Him?

God, in all of His wisdom, love, power, and goodness, has allowed every last painful experience in your life.

Without faith in God's character, we will be unable to understand, appreciate, benefit from, or truly forgive the offenses in our lives.

A Beautiful Life

- What is God's perfect will for you in suffering and offense?

- Why do you respond the way you do to the irritating, unpleasant, and even painful treatment you may receive from others? What are you hoping to achieve?

- Does hurtful and offensive treatment from others motivate you to change and grow, or to complain and feel sorry for yourself? What does this tell you?

- How much has your heart really changed since the day Jesus came into your life? Are you still essentially the same person on the inside (living for fairness, your "rights," legal/performance-based relationships, not knowing or giving grace and love), while appearing "better" outwardly?

- What specific issues of your heart have you learned about so far that might need a major overhaul?

- What specific motives/desires in your heart have hindered or prevented you from truly forgiving others?

• What can you learn from the motivation and responses of the following people?

1. **Joseph** (Gen 50:20)

2. **Job** (Job 1:21-22; 2:10; 13:15)

3. **The Psalmist** (Ps 119:50, 67, 71, 75, 92-93, 107)

4. **Stephen** (Acts 7:60)

5. **Paul** (2 Cor 4:16-18, 11:23-28, 12:7-10; 2 Tim 4:16)

6. **James** (Jas 1:2-4)

7. **Peter** (1 Pet 1:6-9)

8. **Jesus** (Lk 23:34; Phil 2:3-8)

15

LOVED MUCH; LOVE MUCH

Luke 7:36-50

Now one of the Pharisees invited Jesus to have dinner with him, so he went to the Pharisee's house and reclined at the table. When a woman who had lived a sinful life in that town learned that Jesus was eating at the Pharisee's house, she brought an alabaster jar of perfume, and as she stood behind him at his feet weeping, she began to wet his feet with her tears. Then she wiped them with her hair, kissed them and poured perfume on them.

When the Pharisee who had invited him saw this, he said to himself, "If this man were a prophet, he would know who is touching him and what kind of woman she is–that she is a sinner."

Jesus answered him, "Simon, I have something to tell you."

"Tell me, teacher," he said.

"Two men owed money to a certain moneylender. One owed him five hundred denarii, and the other fifty. Neither of them had the money to pay him back, so he canceled the debts of both. Now which of them will love him more?"

Simon replied, "I suppose the one who had the bigger debt canceled."

"You have judged correctly," Jesus said.

"He who
has been forgiven
little loves little."

Luke 7:47b

Then he turned toward the woman and said to Simon, "Do you see this woman? I came into your house. You did not give me any water for my feet, but she wet my feet with her tears and wiped them with her hair. You did not give me a kiss, but this woman, from the time I entered, has not stopped kissing my feet. You did not put oil on my head, but she has poured perfume on my feet. Therefore, I tell you, her many sins have been forgiven–for she loved much. But he who has been forgiven little loves little."

Then Jesus said to her, "Your sins are forgiven."

The other guests began to say among themselves, "Who is this who even forgives sins?"

Jesus said to the woman, "Your faith has saved you; go in peace."

For the following questions, answer either "W" for Woman or "P" for Pharisee.

Of the "sinful woman" and Simon the Pharisee:

_____ Which one was least aware of the extent of his or her sinfulness?

_____ Which one did not know who he or she was, especially in relation to Christ?

_____ Which one was blind to his or her weaknesses and absolute need for a Savior and His love, mercy, grace, and forgiveness?

_____ Which one did not know Jesus?

_____ Which one repeatedly insulted Jesus by his or her inaction, action, and attitude?

_____ Which one lacked joy?

_____ Which one was not, as far as we can tell, forgiven?

_____ Which one doubted the character of Jesus?

_____ Which one doubted the wisdom of Jesus?

_____ Which one did not value or appreciate Jesus?

_____ Which one had an ungrateful heart?

_____ Which one did not understand or appreciate grace, mercy, and love?

_____ Which one was seeking to find his/her life and ended up losing his/her life?

_____ Which one probably thought that he/she deserved heaven?

_____ Which one put his/her hope in their own ability to perform, i.e., "goodness"?

_____ Which one was self-righteous?

_____ Which one had an abundance of self-love?

_____ Which one had lofty self-worth?

_____ Which one had high self-esteem?

_____ Which one probably lived according to the "Fairness Doctrine"?

_____ Which one would be easily accepted and praised by the world's standards?

_____ Which one sought to be accepted and praised by the world's standards?

_____ Which one had his or her heart and behavior belittled when compared to a sinful person?

_____ Which one was devoid of humility and was instead filled with pride?

_____ Which one was selfish, self-centered, and self-focused?

_____ Which one lacked reverence?

_____ Which one would be stuck in his or her old life?

_____ Which one was not esteemed by Jesus?

_____ Most importantly: which one did not _know_ love, as well as _did not love_ ("loved little")?

_____ Which one would have a more difficult experience in forgiving others?

- What conclusions can you draw from your answers to the previous questions?

- How do "high self-esteem," self-importance, and a focus on *self*, help or hinder one's appreciation of: God, others, forgiveness, humility, fruit of the spirit, grace, mercy, and love? Why?

- Does an emphasis on worth, performance, and rights make it easier to forgive others? Why or why not?

16

FORGIVEN MUCH; FORGIVE MUCH

Luke 7:36-50

Take a moment to re-read Luke's account of Jesus' visit to Simon the Pharisee's house, recorded in Luke 7:36-50. Again, of the "sinful woman" and Simon the Pharisee:

(Mark either "W" for Woman or "P" for Pharisee)

_____ Which one was deeply and painfully aware of the extent of his or her own sinfulness?

_____ Which one knew who he or she was, especially in relation to Christ?

_____ Which one was fully aware of his or her weaknesses and absolute need for a Savior and His love, grace, mercy, and forgiveness?

_____ Which one came to know God?

_____ Which one repeatedly blessed Jesus by his or her actions?

_____ Which one overflowed with joy?

_____ Which one was clearly forgiven by Jesus?

_____ Which one trusted Jesus?

_____ Which one cherished, valued, appreciated, worshipped, and glorified Jesus?

_____ Which one had a grateful heart that overflowed with thankfulness?

_____ Which one understood and appreciated grace, mercy, and love?

_____ Which one sought to lose his or her life and ended up finding Life?

_____ Which one lacked any pretension of self-righteousness?

_____ Which one knew he/she deserved hell?

_____ Which one did not put hope in his/her own performance or goodness?

_____ Which one had an _accurate_ assessment of himself or herself, and, therefore, couldn't care less about self-esteem?

_____ Which one gladly gave up living according to the "Fairness Doctrine"?

_____ Which one would not be accepted or praised by the world's standards?

_____ Which one couldn't care less what others might think of him or her, especially compared to what Jesus thought?

_____ Which one had his or her heart and behavior praised by God when compared to the "righteousness" of a religious leader?

_____ Which one was exalted by God because he or she humbled himself or herself before God?

_____ Which one was repentant and turned his or her focus from self to God?

_____ Which one showed reverence?

_____ Which one would experience a new life?

_____ Which one was esteemed by Jesus?

_____ Which one would you enjoy more as a close friend?

The "sinful woman" was painfully aware of her own sin. This is a concept that is taboo for many, as it may hurt one's self-image, self-esteem, or self-worth (i.e., the things cherished by the world); yet it is essential in knowing humility, forgiveness, gratefulness, and eternal life (i.e., the things cherished by God). In losing her life, this woman found Life. By repentance and confession of the truth, she was forgiven. Do you think that she had much difficulty forgiving others after this encounter with Jesus? While the reality of her sin may have been troublesome, she had never known more joy, love, and life! The Truth had set her free!

In contrast, we see the self-righteous Pharisee, praised by the world, yet condemned by God. He was immersed in legal obligations, even with God, rather than loving relationships. Performance, fairness, and the law consumed his heart and life. In seeking his life, he missed out on Life, even when He was in his own home! The deceitful desires of the flesh and the standards of the world imprisoned Simon, perhaps forever!

In losing her life, she found Life.

- Between Simon and the woman, which one knew love, as well as "loved much"? Why?

- Which one would have a more difficult experience with forgiving others? Why?

- Which person in this story do you identify with more? Why?

- Which person would you rather be like? Why?

- What specifically do you need to change?

- What conclusions can you draw from all of your previous answers?

- From what you have read and learned so far, what specifically do you think will help you to more easily forgive others?

- Of the fruit in your own life, how much of it is like Simon the Pharisee's?

- How much of your fruit is like that of "the woman who loved much"?

- Which person had the most potential for a beautiful life? Why?

17

Because there is so much that goes into forgiveness, we need to spend a great deal of time thinking about, meditating on, and verifying through Scripture the beautiful building blocks of grace and mercy.

What follows are several essentials that we need to know, understand, appreciate, and live out if we desire to imitate Christ.

- FORGIVENESS IS: man's greatest need, and, therefore, it is the greatest gift he can receive (Jn 3:16; Lk1:77; Rom 3:23, 6:23). How blessed we are (as well as everyone else) when we too *give* this gift!

- FORGIVENESS IS: *LIFE.* It is the first and most important building block of the abundant and beautiful life. On the other hand, unforgiveness is death and destruction (i.e., separation from God and the absence of life). Essentially and literally, forgiveness is the demarcation between life and death, heaven and hell, blessings and curses (see Deut 30:11-20; 32:45-47).

- FORGIVENESS IS: highly dependent upon love. The more love, the more grace and mercy (Lk 7:36-50; Jn 3:16; 1 Jn 4:16-18). Forgiveness, grace, and mercy all fall under the umbrella of love; they are "subsets" of the divine reality of love. We love only because God first loved us (1 Jn 4:7, 10, 19). Without love we are nothing, have nothing, can do nothing (Jn 15:5; 1 Cor 13:1-3).

- FORGIVENESS IS: directly correlated to the amount of joy, hope, and peace in one's life. The more forgiveness is appreciated and given, the more peace, freedom, joy, and hope we experience (Ps 51; Lk 7:47; Gal 5:22-23).

> Forgiveness is man's greatest need.

> Forgiveness is the first and most important building block of the abundant and beautiful life.

- **FORGIVENESS IS:** being free from the penalty of our offense(s). The sin/offense is not held against us anymore. We are now free to fully enjoy life through God and His love (Is 42:7, 43:18-19; Rom 6:23; Gal 5:1).

- **FORGIVENESS IS:** subject to the character of the offended person, not the quality of the offender. This reality is diametrically opposed to the world's way of thinking. Forgiveness is always undeserved for the person that receives it. Your decision to forgive cannot depend on the offender's worthiness. It is a choice that comes from a broken, humbled, forgiven, loved, grateful, and transformed heart (Acts 7:60). Forgiveness comes out of thankfulness, love, and obedience to God despite what one deserves (Ex 34:9; Num 14:9; Eph 2:3-10; 1 Pet 4:8). Forgiveness is literally "not (prefix: for = not) giving what one deserves." This is the definition of mercy.

  > Forgiveness is subject to the character of the offended person, not the quality of the offender.

- **FORGIVENESS IS:** extremely problematic for the performance oriented person and/or the self-righteous person (i.e., the person who wants to live in the Old Covenant). This person fails to be abundantly horrified at and humbled by the depth of his own sinful heart and behavior (Ps 36:1-3; Lk 18:9-14; cp. Ps 51; Lk 7:36-50). Therefore, he fails to truly appreciate and grasp God's grace and gift. He normally operates outside of grace and mercy, while constantly interpreting and judging the performance of those around him. He finds it very awkward, difficult, even impossible to forgive a failure or weakness (Matt 18:23-35; Lk 7:36-50, 18:9-14).

  > Forgiveness Is a choice that comes from a broken, humbled, forgiven, loved, grateful, and transformed heart.

- **FORGIVENESS IS:** wisdom. The choice and desire to forgive is supremely wise. Forgiveness is pure wisdom "that comes from heaven." On the other hand, refusing to forgive (i.e., "harboring bitter envy and selfish ambition in your heart") is the height of folly and "is earthly, unspiritual, of the devil" (Jas 3:13-18).

- **FORGIVENESS IS:** *not*, as many fear, an open invitation to others to walk all over you. This is neither wise nor loving. Love does not, despite popular teachings of "acceptance" and "tolerance," allow or encourage people to sin by using and/or abusing you. We are to always do what is loving and wise for others. Confronting the sins of others is not only commanded, but it is one way we love one another (Matt 22:29-32; Mk 8:33; Lk 17:3; Jn 3:10-21; Gal 6:1; Eph 4:15, 29; 2 Tim 2:25, 4:2). This, in turn, opens the door for confession, repentance, forgiveness, and reconciliation. Forgiveness is always a part of the bigger goal of love.

  > The choice and desire to forgive is supremely wise.

A Beautiful Life

- **FORGIVENESS IS:** free to the person receiving it. However forgiveness is never free (Mk 10:45; Gal 2:20; 1 Tim 2:6; Heb 9:15; 1 Jn 3:16).

- **FORGIVENESS IS:** acknowledging and confronting, where possible, the sin/offense/debt and choosing to pay the price for the offender's debt. We must recognize sin *as sin* if there is to be any forgiveness. Forgiveness never appeases, ignores, or avoids the offense, but rather, deals with it directly and specifically to get rid of it permanently (e.g., Jesus; Jn 3:16; Eph 2:1-10; Col 1:19-22).

Forgiveness
is not about
rights, fairness,
what we deserve
or what we are
getting out of it.

- **FORGIVENESS IS:** something that always costs the person doing the forgiving, not the person receiving forgiveness. It is a debt paid in full by the person who is owed the debt (Hebrews 9:22). This aspect does not make sense to our flesh or to the world's way of thinking…essentially because forgiveness is not "fair." Yet, in terms of fairness, how much did your forgiveness from God cost you (Rom 6:23; Eph 2:3-10)? And, how much did it cost Him (Matt 26:36-27:50; Jn 3:16, 15:13; Rom 5:8; 8:32; Gal 2:20; 1 Jn 3:16)?

Forgiveness
never appeases,
ignores, or avoids
the offense.
Forgiveness deals
with the offense
directly and
specifically
to get rid of it
permanently

- **FORGIVENESS IS:** not about rights, fairness, what we deserve or what we are getting out of it. Rather, it is about love, mercy, grace and God's glory. Praise God that he did not give us what is fair or what we deserve! Justice comes when the offended person pays (forgives) the debt of the offender. This is not "fair," but it is right. It fulfills our fundamental purpose: it pleases and glorifies God! We are not here to live a fair life, but a life of love that pleases and glorifies Jesus (Matt 5:38-48; Rom 12:1; 2 Cor 5:9; Heb 11:6; 1 Cor 10:31). Fairness does not equal what is right.

We are not
here to live a fair
life, but a life of
love that pleases
and glorifies
Jesus.

- **FORGIVENESS IS:** tremendously complicated, if not impossible, for the person who lives for "fairness" (Old Covenant) in light of God's grace and mercy given to him (New Covenant). This person's hope is in this world—in the world's "wisdom" and mindset, in the performance of others, in working "for food that spoils," as opposed to a hope that is not of this world—in God, His Word, His promises, His love, His kingdom, and an eternity with Him (Ps 62; Jer 2:13, 17:5-8; Matt 6:33). Typically, this mindset's focus and motive is to *get*, rather than to *give* love. "For where your treasure is, there your heart will be also" (Matt 6:21).

- **FORGIVENESS IS:** not eagerly desired, welcomed, or encouraged by our flesh. It abhors grace. Mercy is an abomination. In order to forgive, we must clash against and wage war with our sinful nature. The desire of the sinful nature is to keep you in darkness and enslave you to bitterness. The craving of your flesh is tireless in its "war against your soul" (1 Pet 2:11; see Eph 4:22). The road to victory, freedom, and forgiveness travels through the heart of our selfish, sinful nature. In order to truly love and forgive, we must set our minds/hearts on what the Spirit desires (Rom 8:5-8; 13:14; Gal 5:16; Col 3:1-2), at the expense of our flesh.

- **FORGIVENESS IS:** a golden opportunity to grow and mature in character. This highly desired transformation is achieved when you choose to deny your self, to lose your life, to humble yourself, to cast off concern for self (e.g., self-esteem, self-worth, self-importance, self-image), to put to death the flesh, to be more like Jesus, to walk as Jesus walked, to love God, to love others, and to be esteemed by God rather than man (Is 66:2; Matt 23:5; Rom 8:28-29; 12:1-2; Gal 1:10; Eph 4:31-5:2, 5:15-17; Col 3:5; 1 Thes 2:4). Forgiveness always draws us closer to Jesus. Unforgiveness always drives us away from Jesus (Matt 6:14-15; Job 5:2).

- **FORGIVENESS IS:** God's desire and design for you to transfer your hope from the feeble performance of sinful people and fleeting circumstances and onto the perfect character of God. "Since, then, you have been raised with Christ, set your hearts on things above, where Christ is seated at the right hand of God. Set your minds on things above, not on earthly things" (Col 3:1-2).

- **FORGIVENESS IS:** unlimited. There is no limit to how many times we must forgive a person (Matt 18:21; Lk 17:4). Often, the most difficult forgiveness occurs with the repeated irritating offenses (e.g., "He is never on time," "She always forgets to call back," "They always..."). These (relatively) minor offenses can fly under the radar and easily develop into deep resentment before we know it. This is why we need unlimited grace and love. "Above all, love each other deeply, because love covers over a multitude of sins" (1 Pet 4:8; see also Prov 10:12; 17:9; 1 Cor 13:5).

- **FORGIVENESS IS:** a prime and recurring opportunity to know God, please God, pursue God, put your hope in God, conform to God, obey God, love God, trust God, imitate God, live like God, live in God, and glorify God. Yet how often do we avoid or refuse these frequent and priceless occasions? (See Matt 5:3-16, 5:21-26, 5:38-48, 6:9-15, 6:19-21, 7:1-5, 7:12-14, 7:24-27; 1 Jn 4:7-19.)

- **FORGIVENESS IS:** freedom. It is being free in the present without re-living the hurts of the past (for both sides of the offense). As sinners in a fallen, sinful, and dark world, we long for and need freedom from our sin and the consequences of sin (Ps 119:45; Is 43:18-19, 61:1; Lk 4:18; 2 Cor 3:17; Gal 5:1).

- **FORGIVENESS IS:** not merely forgiving an offense; it is forgiving the *person* who produced the offense (Mk 11:25; Lk 17:3-4, 23:34; Acts 7:60; Rom 5:8).

- **FORGIVENESS IS:** not optional. It is commanded! (See Matt 6:12, 14-15; Mk 11:25; Lk 17:3-4.) Yet, in light of God's love and forgiveness of you, forgiving others is not so much a "have to" as it is a "get to." Truly grasping God's love, grace, mercy, and undeserved gift of salvation (i.e., the New Covenant) makes our forgiveness of others a privilege and an opportunity for even more freedom, blessings, love, and glory to God (Matt 10:8; Lk 7:47; Acts 20:35; Eph 4:32-5:2; Col 3:12-14). A grateful and joyful heart is essential to forgiveness.

- **FORGIVENESS IS:** impossible unless you have the right heart. In order to forgive like God wants you to forgive, your heart needs to be right before Him (Prov 4:23; Matt 6:21, 18:35; Lk 6:35, 23:34; Rom 8:5-8; Acts 7:60; Col 3:1-4; 1 Pet 3:15). *By refusing to forgive, your heart will never be right before God!* (See Matt 6:12, 14-15; Lk 6:37, 11:4.)

- **FORGIVENESS IS:** like love, not based on feelings or emotions, but on God's Word, *His* love, and the forgiveness that He first has for us. The act of forgiveness cannot be based on whether we feel like forgiving or not. Instead, forgiveness must be based on the truth of God's Word—the fact that this is what He desires, and what He asks of us as His children. The intensity of painful feelings cannot determine the choice to forgive. Forgiveness is a commitment to faithfully obey God and His Word (Matt 5:44, 18:32-33; Rom 12:9-21; 1 Jn 3:16, 4:19) no matter how much pain or discomfort we experience. Yet, it is only through God's power that we are enabled to go beyond our feelings and truly forgive.

> In light of God's love and forgiveness of you, forgiving others is not so much a "have to" as it is a "get to."

> Forgiveness is impossible unless you have the right heart.

> The intensity of painful feelings cannot determine the choice to forgive.

- **FORGIVENESS IS**: giving. It is freely giving gifts of freedom, love, grace, clemency, hope, joy, not to mention glory to God. So many of us are focused on, and consumed by, what we are receiving; thus, we fail miserably in forgiving and, ultimately, in God's way of life, which is characterized by love, grace, and mercy. Who is blessed more in forgiveness? Jesus said that it is more blessed to *give* than to *receive* (Acts 20:35).

- **FORGIVENESS IS**: essential to restoring and deepening your relationships (Matt 5:23-24; Lk 17:3; Rom 5:20).

- **FORGIVENESS IS**: a blessing, both for the forgiver and for the one receiving forgiveness (Ps 32:1-2; Lk 7:36-50; 2 Cor 2:7-11).

- **FORGIVENESS IS**: an intentional, aggressive, and persevering act of love (specific examples include: Num 14:9; Ps 25:10-11; Acts 7:60; the life of Jesus). Forgiveness does not spring from passiveness, appeasement, or avoidance.

- **FORGIVENESS IS**: a deep commitment not to talk or think about (dwell on) the offense again (Ps 103:10-13; Jer 31:34; Heb 10:17).

- **FORGIVENESS IS**: viewing the offender through the eyes of love, mercy, and grace rather than through the eyes of performance, guilt, and condemnation (i.e., what *you* judge that they deserve). This can come only from a heart that has been transformed by God's love, mercy, and grace through living in the New Covenant. Again, in order to truly forgive and love others, we need to fully understand the love, mercy, and grace God has for us (the deep reality and significance of the gift of our own salvation) despite what we truly deserve (Ps 51:1, 103:10; Matt 18:23-35; Rom 6:23; Eph 4:31-5:2; Heb 4:15-16).

Forgiveness does not spring from passiveness, appeasement, or avoidance.

Forgiveness is viewing the offender through the eyes of love, mercy, and grace rather than through the eyes of performance, guilt, and condemnation.

HOW DOES THIS APPLY TO ME ?

- What specifically is preventing you from forgiving completely?
  (Check any and all that apply to you)

☐ Lack of knowing, relying on, and giving God's love

☐ Wrong (i.e., selfish/loveless) motives

☐ My pleasure/happiness is more important than God's desire and design

☐ Living for my rights

☐ I live more in "legal associations" with people (rules, regulations, give-and-take expectations, demands, needs), rather than in "loving relationships" (compassion, giving, freedom, generosity, grace, mercy)

☐ Pride

☐ Stubbornness (rebellion)

☐ Ungratefulness

☐ The offense hurts too much (how I feel tends to override God's commands)

☐ Self righteousness…I don't appreciate the depth of my own sinfulness and separation from God

☐ Desire for, insistence upon, and pursuit of "fairness," believing that "forgiveness is not fair"

☐ The condition of my heart…I need to grow and mature in character

☐ My desire for, and pursuit of, self-esteem

☐ I still believe in and follow the world's "wisdom" and its way of handling life's problems

☐ My hope is still in the performance of man (versus the character of God)

☐ My life's experience is dictated by my circumstances (rather than an inner faith in and love for God, no matter what the circumstances)

☐ I do not see, understand, or appreciate God's higher purpose in suffering

☐ I fail to see my own pain and mistreatment by others for the incredible opportunities that they really are

18

Stumbling Blocks To Forgiveness: # 1

There are numerous stumbling blocks that prevent forgiveness. However, given that we have unlimited access to God and His Word, these hindrances are all well within our ability to change and overcome. With that in mind, let's look at some of the biggest problems we, as Christians, face when it comes to forgiveness.

"I thought I forgave him, but I guess I don't know how to forgive."

First, we simply do not know how to forgive.

> This is how my heavenly Father will treat each of you *unless you forgive your brother from your heart.*
>
> Matthew 18:35, italics added

We might say the *words*, "I forgive you," but the reality is we often do not know, understand, or appreciate all that goes into the *process* of forgiveness. On the one hand, forgiving someone is simple. On the other hand, it can be extremely difficult to actually realize true and lasting forgiveness. The amount of difficulty is usually directly related to the severity of the offense.

While there is a required decision to forgive, which is a serious and deep commitment, forgiveness is more of *a series of decisions* to not remember or re-live the original offense. While making this continued choice to forgive may be difficult to do, over time, through practice and a changed heart, it does become easier. Furthermore, the offense comes up less and less in our minds the more often we refuse to re-live and dwell on the offense when it does come to mind. Eventually, this process approaches the much desired "forgive and forget" status.

Whenever we are tempted to remember, talk about, or dwell on an offense it is highly helpful, even essential, that we dwell on our own forgiveness from God. If we are focused on the depth of our sin and separation from God, and therefore the magnitude of His gift of

Forgiveness is more of a series of decisions to not remember or re-live the original offense, and over time, it does become easier.

salvation, it makes it infinitely easier not to dwell on the offenses committed toward us (remember the "sinful woman" from Luke 7?).

However, no matter how much we may know (i.e., the "how to" part), forgiveness is heavily dependent upon a heart changed by God. We need a heart that is growing closer and closer to God's heart. Mercy comes from a heart that knows God's mercy. We can love only if we know God's love (1 Jn 4:7, 10, 19). If we know God's love, then we will truly desire to love Him and others (1 Jn 4:16), specifically through forgiveness (Col 3:13).

Mercy comes from a heart that knows God's mercy.

- On a scale of zero to ten, with ten being a mountain and zero being a molehill, how would you rate this area as a stumbling block to your forgiveness of others?

- Why?

19

I WOULD NEVER!

Stumbling Blocks To Forgiveness: # 2

"I can't believe what he did!"
"I would never do anything like that!"

Second on our list of stumbling blocks to forgiveness is the failure to remember and appreciate the fact that we are *all* sinners. We forget that "there, but for the grace of God, go I."

> For *all* have sinned and fall short of the glory of God.
>
> Romans 3:23, italics added

> There is no one righteous, not even one; there is no one who understands, no one who seeks God. All have turned away, *they have together become worthless*; there is no one who does good, not even one. Their throats are open graves; their tongues practice deceit. The poison of vipers is on their lips. Their mouths are full of cursing and bitterness. Their feet are swift to shed blood; ruin and misery mark their ways, and the way of peace they do not know. There is no fear of God before their eyes.
>
> Romans 3:10-18, italics added

Our deceptive sinful nature tends to produce a prideful, stubborn, and self-righteous attitude rather than a broken, humble, and grateful heart. We need to realize that we *all* have the same horrible condition (sinful hearts that do heinously selfish acts that hurt others—see Rom 3:10-18, 23) and, as a result, we *will be* sinned against, hurt, betrayed, etc., by others our *entire* life.

In addition, we need to acknowledge that we too have hurt others, often deeply and/or repeatedly, by our own sinfulness, selfishness, thoughtlessness, stubbornness, and/or unintended offensive behavior. "If any one of you is without sin, let him be the first to throw a stone at her" (John 8:7; see also 1 John 1:8-10). If you do not see your own sin, you remain in the deepest darkness imaginable (Jn 3:19-20)!

We will be sinned against, hurt, betrayed, etc., by others our entire life.

If you do not see your own sin, you remain in the deepest darkness imaginable.

Understanding that we are all sinners enables us to not take the sin of others so personally. It is not always about you! The reality is, when someone mistreats and hurts you, the problem concerns them much more than it does you. Yet, we have a remarkable propensity to make it more about us.

Remember when the kids in junior high teased you? They could make fun of *anyone* and *everything*. They would relentlessly pounce on any imperfection (real or otherwise). They could taunt you for years concerning the size or shape of your nose, shoes, ears, shirt, teeth, lips, knees, pants, feet, elbows, freckles, fingers, eyes, eye lids, eye lashes, etc? Or maybe they made fun of the way you walked or talked? They might have even ridiculed you about how smart or good-looking you were (this is still my cross to bear, as I'm sure it is yours!).

Looking back, do you see now that their behavior reveals much more about *their* character (e.g., insecurity, insensitivity, selfishness, lovelessness, immaturity, meanness, foolishness, see Prov 22:15) than anything to do with you?

Later in life, even as "adults," not much has changed, has it? People are still, if not more so, insecure, mean, self-centered, rude, unloving, thoughtless, foolish, harsh and, sometimes, downright wicked (see 2 Tim 3:1-4)! There may be some truth to what they are saying (and we need to deal with this truth) but their words and actions are always more indicative of what is going on in *their* hearts and lives than anything to do with you.

This knowledge is essential, valuable, and freeing. Yet, despite God's teachings and warnings, we still focus on our selves! (See Lk 9:23-24, 18:9-14; 1 Cor 13:1-8; 2 Cor 5:15; Phil 2:1-8; 2 Tim 3:2.)

We tend to buy into the worldly emphasis on "high self-esteem" and "increasing your self-worth" and that "the greatest love of all" is love of self. When this happens, we forfeit the truth regarding the accuracy of our standing before God as well as others (again, see Lk 7:36-50). More importantly, we sacrifice the truth by greatly diminishing God's character, especially the quality and quantity of His love.

Is God's manner of love dependent upon our intrinsic value or worth? It is according to the self-esteem idea. Or, does God's love rely solely on His perfect character ("God is love"), *despite our lack of value*? This is the teaching throughout Scripture.

Think of it this way: does Jesus love us because we are so wonderful, or does He love us because He is so wonderful—in spite of our rebellion, darkness, sin, and even hatred of Him (see Matt 5:43-48; Rom 5:6-10; Eph 2:1-10; Ti 3:3-7)? The more *we* are worthy, the less He is worthy to be praised, adored, and glorified!

What would go through your mind if I told you of a man who loved his only child? "Yeah…so…what's the big deal? That happens all the time." Nothing would really stand out about such a man or his character.

But what would you think of a man who loved the murderer of his only child? How often do you see that level of love? Such a love would stand out! More than that, it would be

Others' behavior reveals much more about their character than anything to do with you.

Their words and actions are always more indicative of what is going on in their hearts and lives.

The more we are worthy, the less God is worthy to be praised, adored, and glorified.

A Beautiful Life

remarkable! We would be in awe of this person's character. This is exactly the sort of love, and more, that God has for each of us. It is a love that is based on the wonderful and unfathomable character of God, rather than on anything in or of myself.

Still, the temptation to focus on "self" continues to be strong, and we are told at every turn, *even within the church*, that such an attitude is right and "healthy." Yet this emphasis on self is nothing new. David experienced the same self-absorbed delusion in his day. He revealed the fruit of this mindset when he wrote: "For in his own eyes he flatters himself too much to detect or hate his sin" (Ps 36:2).

The results of this puffed up self-importance and deceit are serious and severe: We lack the fear of God, our words are deceitful and wicked, we cannot appreciate the enormity and significance of our sin, we cease "to be wise and to do good," and we have less and less of a need, desire, or love for God (Ps 36:1-3). Yet, this is precisely what is happening today—*within the body of Christ.*

Without a doubt, these worldly shams are enticing. The tantalizing lies of man strongly appeal to and are easily soaked up by a very willing accomplice—our flesh. For this interaction to succeed, we must set our hope not on what the Spirit desires but on what the sinful nature wants and demands (Rom 8:5-8; Col 3:1-2). Failure to know and follow God's Word results in a failure to comprehend, and therefore hate, the horrific sin in our lives.

The self praising and exalting mentality of humanist thought (man-centered as opposed to God-centered and others-centered) draws our attention away from God and the facts and, instead, to fantasy. This always produces a diminished desire and ability to forgive others from a grateful and loving heart. Why? Because it is about me, not about God, not about others, and not about His kingdom and glory.

The world offers us the proverbial rose colored glasses when it comes to our presumed "goodness." It demands that we think greater, bigger, and better of our selves, no matter what the facts are. In contrast, God's Word never asks us to think higher, but to walk in *reality.* "Do not think of yourself more highly than you ought, but rather think of yourself with *sober judgment*" (Rom 12:3, italics added).

God knows that our problem is that we think too highly of ourselves, at the expense of reality, the fruit of the Spirit, and forgiveness (ours and others). Therefore, He warns us against thinking too highly (*not* too lowly) and commands that we use sober judgment. Why? The painful awareness of your sin and sinful nature is extremely sobering and is the primary and essential step to your salvation! It is also this insight, seeing our ugly sin and the sin of others for what it truly is, that helps so much with compassion, love, understanding, and the forgiveness of others.

The world demands that we think greater, bigger, and better of our selves, no matter what the facts are.

God warns us against thinking too highly (NOT too lowly) and commands that we use sober judgment.

- On a scale of zero to ten, with ten being a mountain and zero being a molehill, how would you rate this area as a stumbling block to your forgiveness of others?

- Why?

20

WHY DID GOD ALLOW THIS?

Stumbling Blocks To Forgiveness: # 3

"I don't see anything good that can come from this."
"Why did God allow this in my life?"
"When will the pain go away?"

We stumble when we fail to see forgiveness as the *incredible opportunity* that it is.

> Make every effort to live in peace with all men and to be holy; without holiness no one will see the Lord. *See to it that no one misses the grace of God* and that no bitter root grows up to cause trouble and defile many.
>
> Hebrews 12:14-15, italics added

> Then he said to them all: "If anyone would come after me, he must deny himself and take up his cross daily and follow me. For whoever wants to save his life will lose it, but whoever loses his life for me will save it."
>
> Luke 9:23-24

> And we know that in all things God works for the good of those who love him, who have been called according to his purpose. For those God foreknew *he also predestined to be conformed to the likeness of his Son*, that he might be the firstborn among many brothers.
>
> Romans 8:28-29, italics added

God obviously commands forgiveness (repeatedly). Yet, we still have a choice. But this is really no choice at all. Think of it like the decision whether or not to stick needles in your eye. Yes, technically you have a choice, but would you choose to go through that excruciating pain?

God's recurring requirement for forgiveness is not His way of attempting to control you or make you uncomfortable.

Rather, it is to free you, empower you, bless you, and transform you—into His image.

God's recurring requirement for forgiveness is not His way of attempting to control you or make you uncomfortable. Rather, it is to free you, empower you, bless you, and transform you—into His image.

The pain, betrayal, and mistreatment in your life are all part of your sanctification (as well as others) and God's glory. God uses the sin of others to work in your life. While others may intend to harm you, God can always use their malice for many blessings as well as glory for Himself (Gen 50:20; Rom 5:3-5, 8:28-29; 2 Cor 1:8-9). What kind of grace, mercy, and growth would you experience without sin, injustice, and unfairness?

What kind of grace, mercy, and growth would you experience without sin, injustice, and unfairness?

All Christians, whether we realize it or not, are in this process of change. Given the nature of our hearts and the fact that we dwell in a dark, sinful, and fallen world, God, in His brilliance, power, wisdom, and love, uses sin and weakness for our growth and His glory (2 Cor 12:9-10). The sins of others and our responses to these offenses are often necessary components to achieve our much needed transformation.

So, we have virtually ceaseless opportunities to die to our selves, to trust God's Word and desire, to avoid needless heartache and misery, to abundantly experience the fruit of the Spirit, to be transformed, to imitate Christ, to love others, to know and experience His power, to impact others for Christ, to re-experience grace and mercy, and, most importantly, to love, please, and glorify God. Your forgiveness of others is the opportunity that accomplishes all of these things.

The sins of others and our response to these offenses are often necessary components to achieve our much needed transformation.

The more mercy is your desire (Matt 12:7), the better God's will is understood (Rom 12:2), and the more you will see forgiving others as the immeasurable opportunity that it is. On the other hand, what opportunities will you have without this fundamental insight and wisdom?

> Be very careful, then how you live—not as unwise but as wise, making the most of every opportunity, because the days are evil. Therefore do not be foolish, but understand what the Lord's will is.
> Ephesians 5:15-17

A Beautiful Life

- On a scale of zero to ten, with ten being a mountain and zero being a molehill, how would you rate this area as a stumbling block to your forgiveness of others?

- Why?

21

IT'S NOT FAIR

Stumbling Blocks To Forgiveness: # 4

"That's not fair!"
"Give me what I deserve!"
"I had it first!"
"I never did that to him!"

A major stumbling block to forgiveness is encountered when we fail to make the transition from the "Fairness Doctrine" to the way of grace, mercy, and love. We try to go back to the Law (Old Covenant/death) when we are under grace (New Covenant/life). No other concept, when understood, appreciated, and lived, will be more impacting and transforming in all areas of your life than the New Covenant—at the expense of the Old Covenant/"Fairness Doctrine." Jesus explained this essential transition in His Sermon on the Mount:

> You have heard that it was said, "Eye for eye, and tooth for tooth." But I tell you, do not resist an evil person. If someone strikes you on the right cheek, turn to him the other also. And if someone wants to sue you and take your tunic, let him have your cloak as well. If someone forces you to go one mile, go with him two miles. Give to the one who asks you, and do not turn away from the one who wants to borrow from you. You have heard that it was said, "Love your neighbor and hate your enemy." *But I tell you: Love your enemies and pray for those who persecute you, that you may be sons of your Father in heaven.* He causes his sun to rise on the evil and the good, and sends rain on the righteous and the unrighteous. *If you love those who love you, what reward will you get? Are not even the tax collectors doing that?* And if you greet only your brothers, what are you doing more than others? Do not even pagans do that? Be perfect, therefore, as your heavenly Father is perfect.
>
> Matthew 5:38-48, italics added

"If you love those who love you, what reward will you get? Are not even the tax collectors doing that?"

Matthew 5:46

Do you remember where you were when you first saw the tragic events of 9/11 unfold, or when President Reagan was shot? How about after President Kennedy was assassinated?

In much the same way, do you remember when you first learned the earth-shattering reality that *life is not fair*?

While this last question is asked somewhat in jest, this fundamental realization, the unfairness of life, can be a traumatic experience for many. And the trauma doesn't stop with just the first realization. Instead, continual injustices are experienced and revisited throughout the rest of our lives.

However, because fairness is so important to some, these painful realities mark precisely where their lives screech to a halt. These injustices act like anchors that hinder or even prevent moving on with many, or all, aspects of their lives (see Heb 12:1-3; Eph 4:31; 2 Sam 13; Jnh 4).

Fairness is the Golden Rule, and the Golden Calf, that is worshipped by the world. With a "feel good about yourself" goal and "good intentions" in hand, those who put their hope in this world cling to fairness as the controlling religion and guiding doctrine of life.

This concept is taught outright in many world religions (e.g., Buddhism, Hinduism, etc.), as well as the "earning your salvation" gospel of every pseudo-Christian cult. In contrast, Jesus taught the so-called golden rule in the positive—meaning, the focus is *not* on what you *receive*, but on what you can *give*. "So in everything, *do to others* what you would have them do to you" (Matt 7:12, italics added; see also verses 9-12, as well as the whole context of chapters 5-7).

For the world, everything is measured by what is fair or unfair. It strives to live by the unwritten *rules* of fairness rather than living for the unseen *Ruler* who is love. For the Christian, whether understood or not, *everything is measured by love*, not fairness.

Contrary to popular thought (i.e., the world's thinking), fairness and love are not the same. Far from it. God's way is, in every aspect imaginable, infinitely superior to the world's dominant yearning (Is 55:8-9).

The world gets to judge what is "fair," with the end result usually favoring the one doing the judging. But the Christian is to trust not in his own heart, feelings, emotions, wisdom or in the world, but in what God has said in His perfect Word. His resounding message is love, no matter how fair or unfair the circumstances (Matt 26-28; 5-7; Lk 23:34; Jn 15:13; Acts 7:60; Rom 5:8).

How often do you hear the complaint of, "That's not fair!"? It is not just on the playgrounds that we hear this mantra, but seemingly in every workplace, sporting event, *church*, and political movement, not to mention within most marriages and family relationships. Wherever there is complaining, gossiping, or bitterness, it is preceded by a wealth of demands for fairness ("fairness" for the complainer, not necessarily for all).

Nearly every book, television, or movie drama captivates us by appealing to our sense of justice. They usually begin with an incident that instinctively offends our "fairness meter." From that moment on, everyone in the audience knows precisely the fate of the offender. In the last fifteen minutes of the movie, or in the last chapter or two of the book, he or she will

Do you remember when you first learned the earth-shattering reality that life is not fair?

Fairness is the Golden Rule, and the Golden Calf, that is worshipped by the world.

God's resounding message is love, no matter how fair or unfair the circumstances.

experience so-called "justice." More often than not, one or more of the victims will get to unleash some sort of excruciating revenge on the offender.

Why is the blueprint of "unfairness-that-ends-in-justice" repeated so often in our stories? Why do we seemingly never tire of this worn-out story line? Because revenge sells! By piquing our interest through unfairness, we are locked into the saga until we *vicariously* experience justice.

How many movies do you see where the "bad guy" gets away? This rarely happens because the writer knows that you detest this kind of ending. Such an ending wouldn't be fair! It would not gratify our lust for revenge.

Fairness is the glorified struggle of the world. Many people dedicate their whole lives to the creeds of fairness. Their heroes are those who demand and fight for what *they* suppose is fair. For them, life is not measured by what is truly right or wrong (i.e., according to absolute truth/God's Word), but solely on their own fuzzy ideas and *feelings* of what is fair or unfair (i.e., according to what they *want* and what they *judge* to be fair).

For the Christian, the real struggle is not between unfairness and what we deem to be fair, but between faith and disbelief, between our flesh and the Spirit, between light and darkness, between God's eternal kingdom and corrupt temporary pleasures, between idolatry and the sufficiency of God, between love and self-love, between sin and grace, between freedom and bondage, between the Old Covenant and the New Covenant, between fixing our eyes on what is seen or on what is unseen, between the sufficiency of God's Word and the "wisdom" of man, between eternal life and never-ending torment in hell.

Our struggle for and focus on fairness diverts our attention from our true and higher calling. This worldly digression effectively excludes our participation in God's kingdom and higher purposes. This is evidenced by the *lack* of love, joy, peace, patience, kindness, goodness, faithfulness, gentleness, and self-control (Gal 5:22-23) that is experienced when we are focused on what is "fair."

Unfairness simply unveils the greater glory to which God has called you. These uncovered realities are *perfect opportunities* to reject the world's way, embrace God's desires, and experience a beautiful life. To *this* are you called, not to the quest for fair treatment.

How does unfairness affect you? What is your typical response when treated contrary to the unwritten rules of fairness? Do you hope for and pursue fairness on earth, or is your life's mission to bring glory to God? Are you seeking temporary earthly benefits or heavenly treasures?

No, you cannot have both. They are mutually exclusive (see the Sermon on the Mount, especially Matt 5:38-48, 6:19-24; Ps 37, 73). However, it is imperative to note: grace and mercy *require* injustice and unfairness (Rom 5:20). You can never have grace without unfairness; mercy is utterly dependent upon injustice.

The reality is, in a sinful and fallen world that is full of darkness, evil, self-absorption, madness, and deceit, we will never have the much sought-after equality and fairness that many passionately chase. Yet, being treated "fairly," getting what we determine we deserve, and protecting and fulfilling our "rights" are often what we live for—even after we have pleaded with God not to receive what we deserve or what is fair and just.

While this may sound harsh, the reality is that those who live for "fairness" tend to be the most stubborn, offended, hurt, complaint-filled, perpetually "victimized" (at least in their mind), angry, depressed, lonely, unhappy, bitter, unpleasant to be in a relationship with, and *unchanging* people on earth. The more consumed they become with "justice" and "leveling the playing field" (usually for their benefit, not others'), the more tunnel vision they develop to the exclusion of God's bigger and better picture.

How concerned with fairness was Jesus in the midst of the "trial" that led to His death? How about Paul and Silas when they were in jail? Stephen when being stoned to death? Joseph when confronted with the brothers that had sold him into slavery? Abraham when asked to sacrifice his son Isaac? How about Shadrach, Meshach, and Abednego when they were thrown into the blazing furnace?

Which sister seemed more concerned with unfairness: Mary or Martha (Lk 10:38-42)? Which woman missed the "one thing," the whole reason for life? What was the resulting contrast in fruit regarding their separate desires and pursuits? Did Jesus respond to Martha's perceived inequity by demanding justice, leveling the playing field, and coddling all who were offended? Why not?

In order to glorify God and live life to the full, not to mention without continual disappointment, anger, resentment, bitterness, etc., we must stop putting our hope in the idea of fairness. This may be a well-intentioned goal, (similar to other noble sounding ideals that look good on paper—such as communism, tolerance, and absolute economic equality), but is it realistic or achievable? More importantly, does God have something far better in mind for us?

This idea of a fair existence sounds great *in theory*, but in reality it is a farce and will never work in the grand scheme of things. Why? As with all of the well-intentioned and "fine-sounding" ideas (Col 2:4), they fail to fully consider the true nature of our hearts, as well as God's surpassing glory and goal for our lives. Instead, these erroneous mindsets have resulted in our current self-absorbed culture, which we could aptly refer to as "The Age of Entitlement."

And it is not just our country that is consumed with this concept. Thanks to rapid increases in technology, our world seems to daily be growing smaller and ever more connected. This fact, combined with more and more emphasis on "globalism," has only helped to spread and empower the "Fairness Doctrine" (see Matt 13:33; 2 Tim 2:17).

More and more, the world is striving for the mutual, universal goal of fairness, in spite of wildly differing opinions as to what the definition of "fair" is. As greater numbers of people rally around this common ambition, the more distracting and divisive fairness will

Do you hope for and pursue fairness on earth, or is your life's mission to bring glory to God?

Grace and mercy require injustice and unfairness.

We must stop putting our hope in the idea of fairness.

become to the pursuit of God, His Word, His kingdom, and the divine ideals of grace and mercy.

There never has been, nor will there ever be, a single society that is fair, let alone a fair world. The United States of America, with all of its weaknesses, is arguably the greatest country in history. Yet, is America fair? No, and it never will be. Even with all of the blessings, "rights," prosperity, and freedom that we *do* enjoy, many people are still miserable.

Why such a lack of joy and peace in the midst of prosperity? Is it the lack of "fairness"? Not at all! That would be missing the point. The depressed existence of many comes not from their circumstances (see Phil 4:6-13; Ja 1:2-4; 1 Pet 1:6-9; Rom 5:1-5), but is determined by their faulty beliefs and misplacement of hope (Ps 17:14, 33:16-17; Is 44:12-20; Jer 17:5-6; Jnh 2:8; Hab 3:17-19; Rom 1:25). They have bet everything, including their existence and experience, on the elusive and bogus premise that sinful people in a sinful world will inexplicably act selflessly and fairly *all* of the time.

Do you really want to gamble your experience in life on the performance of darkened, deceitful, corrupt, and self-centered hearts? Is it wise to risk your enjoyment of life with the same sinful hearts that have repeatedly sinned against you and fall short of God's desires.

How freeing it is to live outside the quest for fairness (i.e., under grace, not the Law)! How liberating to not go up or down depending on something I cannot control. I no longer have to fret over how others think of me and treat me or fear how they might treat me (Ps 37).

Therefore, I am no longer a slave to other's emotions, whims, moods, and sinful behavior. I am free! (Jn 8:32; Rom 8:31-36; Gal 5:1; Ps 119:32) My experience in life is determined by God and my reliance upon Him (i.e., love, trust, obedience) whatever the situation (2 Cor 9:8; Gal 5:13-16, 22-23; Phil 4:11-19).

Paul wrote, "I have learned the secret of being content in any and every situation" (Phil 4:12). What was Paul's secret? It was simply that his hope was not in or dependant upon the situation or circumstances! It was in God—no matter what the situation (Phil 3:7-11, 4:13, 19).

While there is nothing wrong with working toward the betterment of others and "justice for all," the usual result is such that, due to the nature of man, we end up fighting for "fairness" for ourselves! The goal of equality/fairness is not wrong per se, but putting all your eggs solely into the "fairness basket" is a colossal mistake. This inevitably leads to more conflict, injustice, disappointment, offense, hurt, anger, fighting, bitterness, despair, and division.

Which is infinitely greater—God's love or the world's pursuit of fairness? The idea of fairness is at odds with, even at war with, the gospel's themes of faith, sacrifice, servanthood, dying to self, love, freedom, mercy, generosity, humility, grace, patience, and God's glory. Which of these two things—God's love or the idea of fairness—do you desire more? Which one describes your overall mindset and life's pursuit?

The depressed existence of many comes not from circumstances, but is determined by their faulty beliefs and misplacement of hope.

Do you really want to gamble your experience in life on the performance of darkened, deceitful, corrupt, and self-centered hearts?

How freeing it is to live outside the quest for fairness!

Should God's idea of love be the driving force in a Christian marriage, or should that be exchanged for the pursuit of what is fair? The idea of "fifty-fifty" agreement in marriage sounds good, in theory; however, with just a cursory glance at the reality of life and the complexity of our sin, such an ideal crashes and burns worse than the Hindenburg.

What happens to the whole fifty-fifty deal if one spouse is sick? What if the husband is living for God and the wife is an unbeliever? What if one spouse is incapacitated for an extended period of time? Is that fair? Should the other spouse demand equal or special treatment to make up for the previous period of unfairness? That would be only fair, right?

Are we to keep a record of wrongs (1 Cor 13:5)? It would be only fair! But is that love? At what point does God want us to walk out on our spouse because they are not treating us fairly? Yet this is the precise attitude and reasoning behind many divorces today.

In marriage, we make a commitment, "for better or for worse," "in sickness and in health." God knows our tendency, in our sinful nature, to live for and even demand fairness. He also knows this means death to love and marriage. That is why the marriage commitment is so essential.

Living under the "Fairness Doctrine," each spouse would strive to reach the fairness level and then stop. Any more giving would make things "unfair." Does that look like love? Is that how God loves you? Is this how any relationship should work? How many marriages would still exist if we all lived strictly by the "Fairness Doctrine"?

If I live according to my desire for fairness, my approach to marriage will be that I "have to" treat my wife evenhandedly, according to the rules and regulations established. Wow, that sounds like a lot of fun, doesn't it? How much love, peace, and joy would flow from this approach?

If, on the other hand, I follow God's plan and desire, my attitude will not be that I "have to" but that I *get to* love my wife, above and beyond any worldly standard, no matter what she may deserve. Therefore, my treatment of her (i.e., loving actions) will not depend on how well she treats me, but on God's desire and design. How many people would like to be loved like that? Countless lives and marriages would be dramatically transformed if modeled on God's way of love, at the expense of fairness.

If you are or have been married, you know the night-and-day contrast between these two attitudes and their resulting experiences. One is full of conflict, demands, stress, anger, and joylessness. The other, while not devoid of conflict, bears the fruit of love, joy, hope, growth, intimacy, wisdom, and glory to God.

If I view common tasks such as taking out the trash, doing the dishes, even changing diapers(!) as a "have to," then I am missing the point of love, marriage, grace, and life. If, instead, I purposely do even the most mundane chores out of a conscious love for God, my wife, and my family, then even those chores become a "get to" rather than a dreaded duty ("have to"). This outlook changes everything!

Which is infinitely greater: God's love or the world's pursuit of fairness?

Which do you desire more: God's love or the idea of fairness?

How many marriages would still exist if we all lived strictly by the "Fairness Doctrine"?

When has fairness ever really worked? Did it work with The Law (Old Covenant)? Does it work with communism? What has been the overall experience of the majority of people living in communist countries? Can we call the brutal murder of over *one hundred million people* and the terrible oppression of billions more a success (e.g., communist China, the USSR, etc.)? Likewise, how many hearts have been transformed into the image of Christ through fairness?

Whenever someone does get what is fair, it rarely, if ever, gives him lasting happiness or changes his life! Instead, it usually increases his appetite to achieve even more "fairness" in this life (see Prov 27:20; Ecc 5:10, 6:7; Is 55:2; Jer 5:7; Hos 13:6; Jn 6:27). In turn, it also displaces the concept and desire for grace and mercy.

Demanding fairness (like so many do) never transforms a person or a society for the good. Neither does insisting on equality help solve the problem of injustice. Ultimately, it only damages the stated goal and God's purpose.

But impacting and changing hearts through forgiving and giving (2 Cor 8-9), while not demanding to receive, always has God's desired effect. We can only produce this superior end by knowing, relying on, reflecting, and giving God's abundant grace, mercy, and love (1 Jn 4:16-17).

While we can never transform the heart of another, we can *always* love and forgive. When we trust and obey God's desire, we open the door to endless possibilities for change.

Consider the outcome that resulted from the brutal slayings of five missionaries in Ecuador in the mid 1950's. These men, knowing the grave risk they were taking, purposed to share the gospel of Jesus Christ with a remote tribe of South American natives, no matter the personal cost to themselves. Tragically, all five of the men were killed by the very people they sought to bring the knowledge of eternal life to. (For the complete story, see the books "Through Gates of Splendor" and "The Savage My Kinsman.")

In the face of this tragedy, did the young wives of these believers, now suddenly widows, demand justice—as was their right? Were their hearts set on a fair conclusion to this horrific event? Or were they, because of their personal experiences of a merciful and grace-giving God, able to reach beyond justice for something far more noble?

Ultimately, through obedience and faithfulness to God's desire, some of these women were used by God in the colossal transformation of the hearts and culture of the Auca Indians—*the very same people* who had murdered their husbands. Is there any way that the world's insistence on and pursuit of fairness could have accomplished this life changing fruit? Not only did these faithful servants fulfill God's intention, but they ultimately played a huge part in achieving the goal their martyred husbands died attempting to accomplish.

What extraordinary eternal fruit for the kingdom came about through faith, obedience, grace, mercy, and God's love! The "Fairness Doctrine" would have robbed all of us, including the wives, the Aucas, and the watching world, of this beautiful picture of forgiveness and life.

How many hearts have been transformed into the image of Christ through fairness?

Getting what is "fair" displaces the concept and desire for grace and mercy.

While we can never transform the heart of another, we can ALWAYS love and forgive.

If our hearts were to conform to God's heart, if we were to live and teach the way of Jesus (e.g., "It is more blessed to give than to receive." Acts 20:35; Lk 6:32-36, 14:12-14; Jn 15:12-13; 2 Cor 9:6-8), then and only then would our lives, relationships, and society improve. We would even, as only one of many secondary by-products, see greater fairness. But, we would far supersede fairness as a goal in and of itself and realize instead eternal glory and rewards "that far outweigh" (see 2 Cor 4:16-18) anything in this life (i.e., fairness).

Generosity, sacrifice, grace, forgiveness, and love, in whatever circumstance, no matter how we are treated, are always our prime objectives (Matt 5-7; Phil 2:1-11), especially in the face of unfairness. Not only does this please and glorify God, it ushers in power that will ultimately change hearts, relationships, families, churches, and society at large.

Fairness never changes hearts (Rom 8:3), at least not for the better (see Old Covenant/The Law/The Letter; 2 Cor 3:5-15). It is a false hope merely posing as the way to life, especially for the world (see Jn 4:13-14, 6:35, 7:37-38, 8:12, 14:6).

The captivating hoax of fairness masquerades as a magic potion that promises happiness for all; yet, in the end, it devours and destroys all who drink it. Countless people have been and continue to be lured through this "wide gate" and down its "broad path" of hopelessness and destruction (Matt 7:13-15).

Where there is injustice and unfairness, change is always desired. The right kind of change, however, must come from a heart that desires God's glory, and that *His* will be done on earth, just as it is in heaven (His ways, not our ways). In contrast, our self-centered mission is typically only so deep as me getting my "fair share."

Injustice, inequality, prejudice, cheating, and unfairness, while never acceptable, are vital opportunities to forgive, grow in grace, experience God's power, change lives, live in mercy, imitate Jesus, glorify God, and put our hope outside of this world and in God alone.

What is more, "*To this you were called*, because Christ suffered for you, leaving you an example, *that you should follow in his steps*" (1 Pet 2:21, italics added; see also 1 Pet 2:9-23). How did Jesus handle injustice, hate, suffering, and the like? He *entrusted* Himself to God the Father (1 Pet 2:23). So should we!

Indisputably, true unfairness creates true victims. A victim, however, will become either a perpetually enslaved and stunted individual, or he will experience grace, growth, freedom, and the ability to glorify God. Even as innocent victims, we still have a responsibility—a responsibility to forgive! We can forgive and be free. Or we can be confined to, and tortured by, our own choice to remain in everlasting victim-hood.

Why then do so many like to remain victims? For one, believe it or not, it feels good (at least for a little while). Self-pity or pity from others, gained by telling anyone who will listen to you about the injustices in your life, provides a somewhat perverse gratification. Admittedly, there is a certain pleasure in feeling sorry for ourselves or in having someone else pity us.

When we trust and obey God's desire, we open the door to endless possibilities for change.

Generosity, sacrifice, grace, forgiveness, and love, in whatever circumstance, no matter how we are treated, are always our prime objectives.

Fairness never changes hearts, at least not for the better.

A Beautiful Life

We love to hear someone say those captivating words such as …"You poor thing!" or, "I can't believe they did that to you." And for those who choose to be perpetual victims, their lives revolve around such pity-parties. Pity is the currency that makes their world go around.

Another attractive aspect for a perpetual victim is the fact that as long as he is a victim, he does not have to take responsibility. This is a "natural" and burning desire established through the precedent of the original fall of man (see Gen 3:8-13). Both Adam and Eve, when questioned by God regarding their own disobedience, blamed someone else. In the same way, a victim, whether real or perceived, will always have someone or something else to blame. In his mind, it is a kind of "Get Out of Jail Free" card. Ironically, in attempting to shift responsibility and remain a perpetual victim, the reality he experiences instead is one of: "Go directly to jail! Do not pass Go! Do not collect $200!" He is held captive by his own choice.

Blame-shifting is especially handy when we want to cover up our own sin or shortcomings, and can be seen in various forms in the following oft-heard excuses:

> "It's society's fault."

> "My teacher/boss/coach/pastor/neighbor/(whomever)
> just doesn't like me. *That* is why I can't…"

> "The 'man' is keeping me down."

> "My parents didn't love me."

> "I just can't get over what he did to me."

> "If only my spouse had met my emotional needs,
> I wouldn't have had an affair."

> "There is a vast right (or left) wing conspiracy against me."

> "The devil made me do it."

While there can be *some* truth to these justifications, to continually rely on them to excuse our behavior or situation in life is often a worse crime than the original offense!

Some even go so far as to blame God. Yet, in His confrontation of Job, God would have none of this: "Would you discredit my justice? Would you condemn me to justify yourself?" (Job 40:8), are a few of the questions God puts to Job, and to all of us.

Solomon also described our tendency to blame God for our foolishness: "A man's own folly ruins his life, yet his heart rages against the Lord" (Prov. 19:3; see also Gen. 4:5; Is 8:21).

Yet, in spite of the sheer folly of such a position, this is what many of us do when we don't get what we want when we think we should get it. Never mind God's desire that we

"To this you were called, because Christ suffered for you, leaving you an example, that you should follow in his steps."

1 Peter 2:21

Even as innocent victims, we still have a responsibility to forgive!

exercise and grow in faith. Never mind trusting in God's wisdom, sovereignty, power, and love—"I want it now!" When I don't get things my way, "God must be against me!"

Is it fair that thousands, if not millions, of people make more money than you do? Was it fair that Babe Ruth was so good at baseball? Is it fair that some people get married and some don't, or that some couples can have children and some cannot? Is it fair that some people have horrific childhoods, while others grow up with wonderful and loving parents? Is it fair that God made me better looking than you? Is it fair that you are smarter than I am?

So much "unfairness," yet God is in control of it all! Could it be that there is far more going on than we can understand or appreciate? Our job is not to demand an explanation or insist that life make sense to our finite minds (Prov 3:5-6). Our job is to "trust and obey" what we do know…God and His Word. In keeping with this truth, Moses wrote,

> The secret things belong to the Lord our God, but the things revealed belong to us and to our children forever, that we may follow all the words of this law.
>
> Deuteronomy 29:29

When fairness is achieved, however temporary, the highest human aspiration is fulfilled. For the world, that is as good as it gets. Yet, when we overcome unfairness through God's grace, *God's* greatest desire is achieved, which is grace, love, and His glory. How infinitely greater this is than the best that the world can achieve.

Jesus both warned and encouraged us, "In this world *you will* have trouble. But take heart! I have overcome the world" (Jn 16:33, italics added). John echoed Jesus when he wrote:

> This is love for God: to obey his commands. And his commands are not burdensome, for everyone born of God overcomes the world. This is the victory that has overcome the world, even our faith. Who is it that overcomes the world? Only he who believes that Jesus is the Son of God.
>
> 1 John 5:3-5

How miserable and insignificant is the world's highest ambition compared to *anything* having to do with God (see Heb 7:18-19). "For the foolishness of God is wiser than man's wisdom, and the weakness of God is stronger than man's strength" (1 Cor 1:25). To put it another way, we fight over a few lousy crumbs when we could have unlimited access to God's continual feast (Prov 15:15)!

We do not have to be limited and controlled by the sins of others. Instead, Jesus tells us that we are blessed when we are mistreated and persecuted (Matt 5:10-12; 1 Pet 4:13-14). He tells us to rejoice and leap for joy when insulted, hated, and rejected (Lk 6:20-23). Paul even "delighted" in such things (2 Cor 12:9-10)!

Does Jesus condone injustice, inequality, theft, cheating, persecution, or discrimination? Never! Yet, instead of dwelling on the offenses that *will* occur, Christ emphasizes our

"A man's own folly ruins his life, yet his heart rages against the Lord."

Proverbs 19:3

So much "unfairness," yet God is in control of it all!

When we overcome unfairness through God's grace, His greatest desire is achieved.

A Beautiful Life

response to these grievances. How and why you respond the way you do is infinitely more important to Jesus than your fair or good treatment.

Your reaction to injustice always reveals your heart. It unmistakably reveals who and what you are living and fighting for. What does unfairness expose about you? When someone attacks you personally (e.g., through confrontation and/or conflict), he, knowingly or not, is testing your motives, to see how much you really care about him and God's purposes. Unfortunately, our response usually reveals that we care more about ourselves.

Is your hope in this world and in being treated the way you feel you deserve to be treated? Do you see the performance of sinful people as your source of happiness? Or, are you more concerned about loving others despite how well they treat you? Is your hope in the eternal God or in fleeting circumstances? Are you fighting for His kingdom or for yours? Are you living under grace or under the Law? What does the fruit in your life and relationships tell you?

Do you remember what James teaches about the *source* of our fights, quarrels, conflicts, and anger? He said that "they come from *your desires* that battle within *you*" (Jas 4:1ff, italics added; see also Prov 13:10). Your desires. When you don't get what you want, you are more than willing to fight for it. What was your last fight really about? What was so important that you had to fight, even hurt, the person who you are supposed to love?

What is more, James says, your disappointments and anger come from your *wrong motives*—striving to get what *you want* as opposed to what will bless God and others. On top of all this, your hope is in this world, in people, and not in the one Person it should be. As sinful humans, we tend to not seek God, His kingdom, and His righteousness *first*. Instead, we seek first (at best) what is "fair" in our eyes.

However, the good news is: God "gives us more grace" (Jas 4:6), and just when we need it most. The condition to receiving this grace is that we have to do what is not fair—we must humble ourselves! "God opposes the proud but gives grace to the humble" (Jas 4:6). Forgiveness and mercy come at a cost...me. But, I gain Christ instead (Gal 2:20; Phil 3:7-11). Beauty for ashes. Life from death.

How often are people truly objective in what is fair for themselves? Don't we all tend to err on the side of what is best for ourselves? Are sports fans equally as angry and demanding of justice when a referee makes a bad call in their team's favor as they are when the bad call goes against their team? What does this tell you about the nature of our hearts?

Who do you trust to make a fair decision for you? More importantly and more to the point, who do you trust to decide what is *best* for you? Is your faith in God, in His wisdom, sovereignty, love, and absolute goodness; or is your faith in yourself, with your finite mind, and selfish and corrupt sinful nature?

To what extent do you trust the world, its "wisdom," and its utmost passion for, and pursuit of, fairness? As we have seen, the "Fairness Doctrine" is cherished by man; yet, *"what is highly valued among men is detestable in God's sight"* (Lk 16:15, italics added).

How and why you respond the way you do is infinitely more important to Jesus than your fair or good treatment.

Is your hope in this world and in being treated the way you feel you deserve to be treated?

Forgiveness and mercy come at a cost...me. But, I gain Christ instead.

We must make the necessary transition from "fairness" to mercy, grace, love, and God's glory. Forgiveness is God's design to transplant your hope from the performance of people to the glory of God!

With fairness as the grand goal, we are surrounding ourselves with *legal obligations* rather than committed and *loving relationships*. In living for fairness, the relationships in our lives become more like contractual duties where both parties demand satisfaction—or else! What is more, our contracts (established to favor ourselves and our own desires) will frequently conflict with another's (established to favor themselves). This is when fights occur (Jas 4:1-3). At best, we agree to a cease fire or we amend our contracts through some form of temporary peace treaty.

Either way, we are constantly looking for the loopholes like any good lawyer would do. We are ruled by rules, regulations, demands, and the law. But if someone tries to call *us* on a loophole, we tenaciously stick to and fight for the letter of the law (2 Cor 3:6).

However, as a Christian, you must realize that when you plead for God's mercy, love, and grace, you are, intentionally or not, giving up on the hope for, and pursuit of, fairness. You must tear up the imaginary "Fairness Contract" and renounce your pledge to the idea of fairness.

By trusting Christ, you are entering into the New Covenant (Matt 26:27-28; 2 Cor 3:5-18; Heb 7:19, 7:22, 8:6-13, 9:11-14). The promise is first and foremost between you and God. You agree to entrust all to Him. Everything in this covenant is based on, surrounded by, and for the purpose of God, His love, grace, power, Word, kingdom, and glory—*not yours*. In this new agreement and arrangement with God you are essentially saying the following:

> "I, _____ , hereby do gladly agree and commit to living by grace, love, freedom, forgiveness, and God's power, while, just like Christ, entrusting all my rights, unfair treatment, and circumstances, good and bad, over to God. Unfairness, mistreatment, offenses, and injustices are now divine opportunities to re-live God's love, grace, and mercy; to impact others for the kingdom of God; to grow and mature; to conform to the image of Christ; and to glorify God. My hope is no longer in the performance of sinful man or in the corrupt ideas and desires of the world but in the perfect character of God."

Not that we are competent in ourselves to claim anything for ourselves, but *our competence comes from God.* He has made us competent as ministers of a *new covenant*--not of the letter but of the Spirit; *for the letter kills, but the Spirit gives life.*

2 Corinthians 3:5-6, italics added

Forgiveness is God's design to transplant your hope from the performance of people to the glory of God!

You must tear up the imaginary "Fairness Contract" and renounce your pledge to the idea of fairness.

"For the letter kills, but the Spirit gives life"

2 Corinthians 3:6

This understanding and commitment is essential to changing your heart, mindset, and purpose so that your daily experience will be changed, as well as every relationship you have. Moreover, "you may participate in the divine nature" (2 Pet 1:4), while avoiding much needless heartache and corruption.

Without this commitment and appreciation, your fruit will be bitter and your forgiveness problematic. In contrast, following this new way of living, you will be free. Free to forgive. Free to live. Free to know God intimately. Free to trust God. Free to glorify God.

- On a scale of zero to ten, with ten being a mountain and zero being a molehill, how would you rate this area as a stumbling block to your forgiveness of others?

- Why?

22

YOU DON'T KNOW

Stumbling Blocks To Forgiveness: # 5

"You don't know the excruciating pain I have been through."
"How can you expect me to forgive all that has been done to me?"

We will stumble in forgiving others when we fail to appreciate, know, and *trust* God's character, especially in suffering.

> And you have forgotten that word of encouragement that
> addresses you as sons:
>
> "My son, do not make light of the Lord's discipline,
> and do not lose heart when he rebukes you,
> because *the Lord disciplines those he loves,*
> and he punishes everyone he accepts as a son."
>
> *Endure hardship as discipline; God is treating you as sons.*
>
> Hebrews 12:5-7, italics added

This is how we are saved in the first place (belief/faith/trust), as well as how we are called to have faith in Christ every moment of every day (Rom 14:23; Gal 5:6; Heb 11:6)! How much more is faith in God essential in times of hardship? We must always keep in mind that God, in His love, goodness, wisdom, faithfulness, and power, has allowed the painful experiences in our lives. "In faithfulness you have afflicted me" (Psalm 119:75).

Joseph's attitude toward his brothers (who deeply and horrifically betrayed him) reveals a heart that, even through unimaginable pain, fully trusted God's wisdom, sovereignty, love, and plan for his life, as well as for many others. Years later, when face-to-face with the same brothers who had betrayed him, Joseph tells them, "You intended to harm me, but God intended it for good to accomplish what is now being done, the saving of many lives" (Gen 5:20).

We must always keep in mind that God, in His love, goodness, wisdom, faithfulness, and power, has allowed the painful experiences in our lives.

In fact, God esteems our trust in Him so highly that one of His chief purposes in our anguish is to increase our faith in and dependency upon Him. Highlighting this truth, Paul writes to the believers at Corinth:

> We were under great pressure, far beyond our ability to endure, so that we despaired even of life. Indeed, in our hearts we felt the sentence of death. *But this happened that we might not rely on ourselves but on God.*
>
> 2 Corinthians 1:8-9, italics added

When you are offended and hurt by another, always keep in mind God's big picture, His grand agenda…for you, for others, and for His kingdom and glory.

God is working on your heart, to draw you closer to Him, to know Him more, to need Him more (faith), to love Him (and others) more, and to be like Him more and more (Rom 8:29; 2 Cor 3:18; Phil 3:10-11; Jas 1:2-4). But, in order to take advantage of suffering, you must trust in His perfect, all-powerful, all-loving character!

> In order to take advantage of suffering, you must trust in God's perfect, all-powerful, all-loving character.

With this perspective in hand, try to see and understand the painful experiences in your life, past and present, in a different way. Knowing God's character allows us to make sense of everything in life, especially suffering. Without it, we are blind and lost.

Suppose you knew in advance that someone was going to knock you out, take hold of a sharp knife, and cut your body open with it. What is more, once you were cut open, he planned to poke, prod, and cut your body for several hours until he was satisfied. After he was done on the inside, he would then grab a huge needle and repeatedly pierce your body with it.

If you were aware that this was what was going to happen to you on a given day, wouldn't you want to run away as far as you could and hide in the best place possible? Yet, every day thousands of people volunteer to go through just such an ordeal as I've described above. Why? Simply because they understand the plan and purpose behind the painful procedure known as surgery.

> Knowing God's character allows us to make sense of everything in life, especially suffering.

The reality is that no matter how you look at it, whether you want it or not, the aching, throbbing, and soreness you feel as a result of surgery will be precisely the same. However, your attitude and understanding of what is happening will make all the difference in your experience, both before and after.

If you fully appreciate that the operation is for your benefit, even to save your life, you might not be able to wait for it to happen. With this vital knowledge, you will be more than willing to undergo this necessity.

The same insight and appreciation is needed to understand the surgery that God must do on your heart. Either way, He is going to do it. You are going to feel precisely the same amount of pain. But your trust in His wisdom, power, and love make all the difference. This will, in turn, greatly affect your willingness and ability to forgive and grow.

Consider the following verses that help illuminate God's bountiful purposes in your troubles and affliction...

Therefore, since we have been justified through faith, we have peace with God through our Lord Jesus Christ, through Whom we have gained access by faith into this grace in which we now stand. And we rejoice in the hope of the glory of God. Not only so, but *we also rejoice in our sufferings, because we know that suffering produces perseverance; perseverance, character; and character, hope. And hope does not disappoint us, because God has poured out His love into our hearts by the Holy Spirit, whom He has given us.*

Romans 5:1-5, italics added

That is why I am suffering as I am. Yet I am not ashamed, because I *know* Whom I have *believed*, and am *convinced* that *He is able* to guard what I have *entrusted* to Him for that day.

2 Timothy 1:12, italics added

God disciplines us for our good, that we may share in His holiness...without holiness no one will see the Lord.

Hebrews 12:10, 14, italics added

Consider it pure joy, my brothers, whenever you face trials of many kinds, because you know that *the testing of your faith develops perseverance.* Perseverance must finish its work *so that you may be mature and complete, not lacking anything.*

James 1:2-4, italics added

How essential is your faith?

> *Everything* that does not come
> from *faith* is sin.
> Romans 14:23, italics added

> The *only thing* that counts is *faith*
> expressing itself through love.
> Galatians 5:6, italics added

> *Without faith* it is *impossible*
> to please God.
> Hebrews 11:6, italics added

Are God's will, desire, and purpose for you more important and desirable than getting what you want when you want it? How willing are you to be mistreated by others if it brings about conformity to the image of Christ? How desirous are you to undergo trials if they result in "praise, glory, and honor" for Jesus (1 Pet 1:6-9; Jn 11)?

The right answers to these questions will help you move in the right direction in regard to forgiveness.

"The only thing that counts is faith expressing itself through love."

Galatians 5:6

- On a scale of zero to ten, with ten being a mountain and zero being a molehill, how would you rate this area as a stumbling block to your forgiveness of others?

- Why?

23

Stumbling Blocks To Forgiveness: # 6

"I need love, acceptance, security, respect, happiness…"
"I need, I need, I need!"

Another significant stumbling block to forgiveness is that we fail to know, experience, and value the love of God, and to give this same love to God and others. When God (specifically, His love) is viewed as *insufficient*, we are not content. Therefore, we believe we "need" (or lack) that which He has already given us in abundance.

> And God is able to make *all* grace *abound* to you, so that in *all* things at *all* times, *having all that you need*, you will *abound* in *every* good work.
>
> 2 Corinthians 9:8, italics added

Instead of living in God's love and grace, we are too easily preoccupied by, and consumed with, pursuing "love" from anything outside of God (see *Chapter 21* regarding the concept of the "Fairness Doctrine," and *Chapter 25* regarding the "bogus gospel"). This gullibility and foolishness is at the root of an empty and barren life.

> This is what the Lord says:
> "Cursed is the one who trusts in man, who depends on flesh for his strength and *whose heart turns away from the Lord*. He will be like a bush in the wastelands; he will not see prosperity when it comes. He will dwell in the parched places of the desert, in a salt land where no one lives."
>
> Jeremiah 17:5-6, italics added

Jesus described it this way…

> The worries of this life, the deceitfulness of wealth and the desires for other things come in and choke the word, making it unfruitful.
>
> Mark 4:19

When God (specifically His love) is viewed as insufficient, we are not content.

This fleshly divergence exemplifies our walking by sight and not by faith (2 Cor 5:7). We essentially live a life of putting our hope in people, their performance, man's "wisdom," and temporary circumstances, all in the anticipation that they will make up for what we perceive to be God's "lack."

The gospel, the true gospel, represents the exact opposite of this strategy. Paul and Barnabas shouted to all who could hear, "We are bringing you good news, telling you to *turn from these worthless things to the living God*" (Acts 14:15, italics added).

What is our life like when our hope in is God alone? Jeremiah contrasts the desert experience (Jer 17:5-6) with the abundance of the fruit of life:

> But blessed is the man who trusts in the LORD, whose confidence is in him. He will be like a tree planted by the water that sends out its roots by the stream. It does not fear when heat comes; its leaves are *always* green. *It has no worries in a year of drought and never fails to bear fruit.*

> Jeremiah 17:7-8, italics added

We may label our desires or lusts as "needs," yet this word is often just a code word for the idols we worship in our hearts.

However, when we feed our selves (the flesh) at the trough of the world, our normal desires and/or worldly and deceptive cravings grow and grow until they are out of control. We convert our everyday wants into lusts, expectations, and demands. This effectively strains relationships, pushes people away, and separates us from God. We may label our desires or lusts as "needs," yet this word is often just a code word for the idols we worship in our hearts.

And as if this destruction were not enough, all of this misplaced hope and trust comes at the costly expense of our only true hope (i.e., in God, His Word, and His kingdom). If anger, bitterness, fighting, and depression reside where the fruit of the Spirit should, then, chances are, your hope is placed somewhere outside of God, His love, and His kingdom.

When we subscribe to the world's way of thinking, we are saying that God and His love are not enough.

The undeniable reality is that when we subscribe to this way of thinking and living, we are saying that *God and His love are not enough*! (See Ps 23; Jer 17:8; Is 55:1-2; 2 Cor 9:8; Eph 3:19-20; Phil 4:19; Col 2:10; 2 Pet 1:3-4.) Instead of pursuing and knowing God and His unending love, and thereby being able to freely give this same love, we live a life fixated and dependant upon receiving (demanding) "love" from the things of this world.

Continually hoping in that which is "broken" (i.e., people and things) and unable to provide for one's needs will always lead to separation from God, unfruitfulness, despair, and full-blown misery. If this misplacement of hope applies to you, not only will you be perpetually offended, hurt, and angry, but it will be exceedingly difficult for you to truly forgive.

Knowing and, therefore, giving God's love is the key to true forgiveness and a beautiful life.

Knowing, and therefore giving, God's love is the key to true forgiveness and a beautiful life. This is how we change our heart. What can transform you more than God's love? If you cannot be content with God alone, how can faulty, weak, foolish, sinful, selfish man make up for God's perceived lack? There is no single area that impacts your life more than what you believe concerning the abundant sufficiency of God (see *Chapter 21* regarding the New Covenant).

> "Martha, Martha," the Lord answered, "you are worried and upset about many things, *but only one thing is needed.* Mary has chosen what is better, and it will not be taken away from her."

Luke 10:41-42, italics added

- On a scale of zero to ten, with ten being a mountain and zero being a molehill, how would you rate this area as a stumbling block to your forgiveness of others?

- Why?

24

Stumbling Blocks To Forgiveness: # 7

"The pain is too much!"
"It is an insurmountable obstacle."
"I don't want to re-live the agony."
"You have no idea how much I have been through."
"The forgiveness process is too difficult."

Many of us stumble when it comes to forgiving others because it is seemingly too painful. We have a very understandable aversion to pain. Furthermore, we usually lack the desire and wisdom to handle the uncomfortable and painful experiences in life. Consequently, we are often doomed to repeat the same discipline/suffering until we are "trained by it."

> No discipline seems pleasant at the time, but *painful*. Later on, however, it produces a harvest of righteousness and peace *for those who have been trained by it*.
>
> Hebrews 12:11, italics added

"Everyone undergoes discipline" (Heb 12:8), but not everyone is "trained by it." What makes the difference? The key is one's *response* to suffering, correction, and discipline. This is revealed in the last eight words of the verse: *"for those who have been trained by it."*

No one likes the sensation of pain, yet God, in His love and wisdom, designed us to experience pain. No one likes to be hurt or uncomfortable, yet this is often when the greatest growth occurs.

Pain is painful; there is no way around it. But pain has a godly purpose (Heb 12:5-11; Rom 5:1-5; Phil 3:10-11; Jas 1:2-4; 1 Pet 1:6-9). With this divine appreciation you can deal with hardship head-on so that you can move on, grow, and be free. Without this understanding you will try to avoid, appease, and dilly-dally around the difficulties in life. Choosing this way, will leave you limited and controlled by your pain—sometimes forever!

We can choose to either be someone who is "trained" through the difficulties of life, or we can resist and resent God's discipline, thereby avoiding the promised "harvest of

No one likes to be hurt or uncomfortable, yet this is often when the greatest growth occurs.

Pain has a godly purpose.

righteousness and peace." What is more, by choosing the latter, we may have to experience the same hardship again and again—until we *do* learn!

Growing up near the beach, I quickly learned to tell the difference between the tourists and the locals, simply by the way they approached the art of body surfing (okay, maybe it was their tan lines as well). When it came to body surfing, there was an easily observable distinction between foolish inexperience and that of wisdom learned through experience.

The visitor or novice gradually wades into the cold water with the hopes of eventually finding the right place to catch a wave. He needlessly prolongs the dreaded acclimation to the sometimes freezing cold water. I am sure that this tactic makes perfect sense to the tourist, but it is truly an unnecessary and miserable experience. While inching along with chattering teeth, he struggles to get past the initial set of waves. He tries to somehow get around these waves but, instead, receives continual setbacks to his overall quest. Eventually, after being frozen and battered around for what seems an eternity, he reaches his desired destination (of course, actually catching a wave is another painful issue!).

This inexperienced and ill-advised line of attack mirrors the method of many in their approach to conflict and the process of forgiveness. And, like inexperienced surfing, forgiveness does *not* have to be so prolonged and painful!

In stark contrast, the approach that the seasoned veteran takes to body surfing probably seems insane to the rookie, at least at first. The veteran already knows from experience that the water *will be* cold and uncomfortable, while the waves will relentlessly thwart his advances. Wisdom also tells him that he cannot control or change the temperature or the force of the waves. However, he knows that he *can* alter his attitude and approach and, therefore, his experience and success.

With this in mind, the local makes a beeline straight for the waves. He sprints as far as he can until confronted with the first significant wave. In a move that seems, at least to the uninitiated, crazy, he dives head first, just under the wave. His momentum gained from the sprint takes him easily beyond the turbulence to the calm of the other side. This is precisely where he needs to be in order to experience the joy of riding the waves.

Again, this appears crazy and believe me, it is not comfortable. In fact, it is quite a shock to your body. Yet it is an exhilarating jolt like no other. What is more, within a few seconds, you are quickly acclimated to the cold water and you are exactly where you want to be. You are now free to do what you came to do.

Furthermore, the wiser and more experienced body surfer has several wonderful experiences before the vacationer even has one. On top of this, even that one experience for the novice is a cold and miserable one.

The tourist may look at the local's approach and think "Wow! That is painful. He's crazy! Whatever I do, I am not doing *that*." Yet, what the tourist fails to realize is that there is no way to avoid the pain and discomfort of the water and waves. It is one's *approach* to the inevitable that makes all the difference.

It is one's attitude and approach to the storms of life that will make all the difference.

Are you an avoider when it comes to approaching the pain of the past and your responsibility to deal with it in the present?

In the same way, pain is inevitable in every person's life. And here too, it is one's attitude and approach to the storms of life that will make all the difference. We can attack the storms head on, or we can prolong our misery. We can be free and enjoy life, or we can be battered around—limited and controlled by our unwise and undisciplined mindset.

The forgiveness process will be uncomfortable. Experience tells us this much. Wisdom tells us that if we approach it head on, with the right attitude, we will come out on the other end right where we want and need to be. This unnatural and unworldly approach (i.e., discipline) brings freedom and joy to life, no matter what the conditions.

Are you an avoider, a novice, a tourist when it comes to approaching the pain of the past and your responsibility to deal with it in the present? Or do you, by faith, wisdom, discipline, and maybe some experience, run right at difficulties and responsibility, thereby experiencing the fruit of God's design?

The uncomfortable, sometimes agonizing, process of forgiveness is our only true hope of dealing with, ridding ourselves of, and growing from the pain of the past. Yet, many of us make it far more difficult than it needs to be.

- On a scale of zero to ten, with ten being a mountain and zero being a molehill,
  how would you rate this area as a stumbling block to your forgiveness of others?

- Why?

25

I DESERVE . . .

Stumbling Blocks To Forgiveness: # 8

"You deserve to get all you can in this life."
"You can't love others until you first love yourself."
"You need others to fill your 'love tank.'"
"God guarantees healthy bodies and happy circumstances."

We stumble over forgiveness when we buy into and sign up for a tainted, worldly, *me-centered*, and therefore, bogus gospel. There is no good news when we fall for the "wisdom" and desires of the world.

> I know that after I leave, savage wolves will come in among you and will not spare the flock. *Even from your own number men will arise and distort the truth in order to draw away disciples after them.* So be on your guard!
>
> Acts 20:29-31, italics added

> One sinner destroys much good.
> As dead flies give perfume a bad smell,
> so *a little folly outweighs wisdom and honor.*
>
> Ecclesiastes 9:18-10:1, italics added

> My people are destroyed from lack of knowledge.
> A people without understanding will come to ruin!
>
> Hosea 4:6, 14

> Blessed is the man
> who does not walk in the counsel of the wicked
> or stand in the way of sinners
> or sit in the seat of mockers.
> But his delight is in the law of the LORD,
> and on his law he meditates day and night.
> He is like a tree planted by streams of water,

There is no good news when we fall for the "wisdom" and desires of the world.

"A little folly outweighs wisdom and honor."

Ecclesiastes 10:1

which yields its fruit in season
and whose leaf does not wither.
Whatever he does prospers.

Psalm 1:1-3

Many people are presented with, and/or accept, a *feel good* "gospel" that leaves out the hard facts and harsh realities of sin, suffering, and sanctification. In the rush to get people in the door and "saved," many leave out the whole gospel, which contains such realities as: "For it has been granted to you on behalf of Christ not only to believe on Him, *but also to suffer for Him*" (Phil 1:29, italics added).

When we buy into a diluted, attractive-to-our-flesh sort of message, not only are we deceived with a false gospel, we will then be untrained, unprepared, and overwhelmed when we sin or someone sins against us. By believing the world's counsel, we are ill-equipped to understand, or respond, according to God's design and desire.

Yet, modern psychology has so permeated the church that it has taken over the gospel for many. When falsehood moves in, the truth moves out.

> For the time will come when men will not put up with sound doctrine. Instead, *to suit their own desires*, they will gather around them a great number of teachers *to say what their itching ears want to hear*. They will turn their ears *away from the truth* and *turn aside to myths*.

2 Timothy 4:3-4, italics added

The results of exchanging the truth of God for the lies of the world are subtly, yet clearly, seen. Worldly ideas are embraced and ushered in; as a result, God's truth is pushed out.

- Victimization is in. **Responsibility** is out.

- "Illness" is in. **Repentance** is out.

- Self-esteem is in. **Humility** is out.

- "Rights" are in. **Righteousness** is out.

- Hopelessness from oppressive "diseases" and "disorders" is in. **Hope** for transformation and a new life are out.

- Permanent conditions (e.g., "once an alcoholic, always an alcoholic") are in. **The new creation and a new heart** is out.

- Fleeting happiness/fulfillment is in. **Holiness** is out.

- Self is in. **God** is out.

By believing the world's counsel, we are ill-equipped to understand, or respond, according to God's design and desire.

When falsehood moves in, the truth moves out.

My "misbehavior" is now my well-intentioned, naïve, and innocent attempt to meet my "legitimate, God-given needs."

- Dependency on programs, people, groups, man's "wisdom," "psychobabble," pills, and therapists is in. **Dependency on God and His Word** is out.

- Satisfying relationships are in. **Godly relationships** are out.

- "Needs" are in. **Freedom and the sufficiency of God** are out.

- Finding your life is in. **Losing your life** is out.

- Fairness is in. **Forgiveness** is out.

Sin, selfishness, and crimes are now "deficiencies," "diseases," and "disorders." Therefore, I am no longer responsible for what I do or how I respond. If I am not answerable for my actions, then I do not have to repent. If I do not need to repent, then there is no hope and no transformation.

According to the popular needs/deficiency model, whatever used to be called sin is now a disorder and/or a disease that results from *other people* not meeting my "needs" (creating deficiencies). As a result, all of the Bible verses describing my sinful heart and propensity to sin no longer apply. The actual sin in my life is no longer sin.

But notice that Jesus said (as well as Moses, Solomon, Jeremiah, etc.) that my sinful behavior comes from my sinful heart.

> For from within, *out of men's hearts*, come evil thoughts, sexual immorality, theft, murder, adultery, greed, malice, deceit, lewdness, envy, slander, arrogance and folly.
>
> Mark 7:21-22, italics added

Yet psychologists freely and unashamedly contradict Jesus by teaching that my "misbehavior" is now my well-intentioned, naïve, and innocent attempt to meet my "legitimate God-given needs." With this belief, who can blame me? (Notice the implied blame on God and others for my behavior/sin, and not myself?)

Why should I repent and change? It's not my fault. I don't need forgiveness. If only *others* would _____ then I wouldn't do _____ . My goal in life is now to get others to gratify my desires (i.e., manipulation) rather than to trust, please, love, conform to, and glorify God.

Have you noticed that what used to be a child's disrespect, disobedience, foolishness, and outright rebellion now conveniently fits under various "disorder" labels? What the Bible calls gluttony, lack of self-control, selfishness, and idolatrous pursuits of pleasure are now diseases or illnesses. It is difficult, if not impossible, to apply confession, repentance, mercy, and grace to a disease or disorder.

It seems there are new "disorders" invented everyday. The overabundance of these unfortunate and misleading labels serve mainly to distort and dilute the very real problems

It is difficult, if not impossible, to apply confession, repentance, mercy, and grace to a disease or disorder.

If I am not answerable for my actions, then I do not have to repent. If I do not need to repent, then there is no hope and no transformation.

that humans struggle with. The fallout from the worldly gospel is that we are robbed of truth, responsibility, hope, faith, obedience, transformation, fruit of the Spirit, and glory to God.

"I can't help it, my disorder (or disease or deficiency) *made me* do it." I have a built-in and permanent excuse for anything I do. With this worldly belief, my hope is not in God, His Word, repentance, discipline, or faith and obedience. My sole hope for life is now in modern psychologists. Hmmmm . . .

God's Word and His beloved have been under vicious attack since day one ("Did God really say…?" Gen 3:1). The Bible is bursting with warnings about false teachers, opposing ideas, wolves in sheep's clothing, the spirit of the antichrist, false prophets, etc., and yet, even with all of these dire admonitions, the church seems extraordinarily at ease in the world.

The approval and teaching of man's "wisdom," in defiance of God's Word, by many within the church is astonishing! What does God say about this teaching that opposes His? "Where is the wise man? Where is the scholar? Where is the philosopher of this age? *Has not God made foolish the wisdom of the world*?" (1 Cor 1:20, italics added) "*For the wisdom of this world is foolishness in God's sight*" (1 Cor 3:19, italics added; see 1 Cor 1:17-3:23).

So, in light of the truth, the abundant sufficiency of God's Word, and His repeated warnings within His Word, all contrasted with the foolish, corrupt, deceptive, godless, and destructive nature of the world's thinking, are we to believe that those who reject, and even hate, God and His Word have essential teachings for our lives that God has failed to give us?

Does anyone see a problem with this? Apparently the apostle Peter did. Therefore he encouraged his readers, including us, when he wrote:

> *His divine power has given us everything we need for life and godliness through our knowledge of him* who called us by his own glory and goodness. Through these he has given us his very great and precious promises, so that through them you may participate in the divine nature and escape the corruption in the world caused by evil desires.

> 2 Peter 1:3-4, italics added

Paul encouraged the church at Colosse with the same beautiful truth concerning God and His Word:

> My purpose is that they may be encouraged in heart and united in love, so that they may have the full riches of complete understanding, in order that they may know the mystery of God, namely, *Christ, in whom are hidden all the treasures of wisdom and knowledge.*

> Colossians 2:2-3, italics added

Are we to believe that those who reject, and even hate, God and His Word have essential teachings for our lives that God has failed to give us?

"His divine power has given us EVERYTHING we need for life and godliness through our knowledge of him."

2 Peter 1:3

After establishing the sufficiency of God and His Word, Paul immediately warns us of precisely what happens every day within the church:

> I tell you this so that no one may deceive you by fine-sounding arguments. See to it that no one takes you captive through hollow and deceptive philosophy, *which depends on human tradition and the basic principles of this world rather than on Christ.*
>
> Colossians 2:4, 8, italics added

In the very last letter which he would ever write, Paul exalts the supremacy and fullness of the Word to his beloved disciple:

> All Scripture is God-breathed and is useful for teaching, rebuking, correcting and training in righteousness, so *that the man of God may be thoroughly equipped for every good work.*
>
> 2 Timothy 3:16-17, italics added

Is God's Word sufficient? Is it deficient? If it is "everything we need for life and godliness," why then do we run to the world? When we believe in the foolishness of the world, we are effectively rejecting the sufficiency of the Word.

The philosophies of man will always appeal to our flesh. They sound so good to our sinful nature. These ideas are charming, but only to the part of us that loves darkness. They are enticing and fascinating, but, in reality, they are dark, deadly, and anti-God.

> This is the verdict: Light has come into the world, but men loved darkness instead of light because their deeds were evil. *Everyone who does evil hates the light, and will not come into the light for fear that his deeds will be exposed.* But whoever lives by the truth comes into the light, so that it may be seen plainly that what he has done has been done through God.
>
> John 3:19-21, italics added

How grievous it must be to God when we don't put up much of a fight over even the most highly suspicious and dubious worldly thinking. Often, it seems our only requirement is that the teaching be popular. If it's all the rage, if enough people like it, if it sells books, if it gets people in the door, if it sounds good in theory, and, most importantly, *if it makes me feel good*, then it *must* be true and, therefore, no Biblical test is needed.

> But I am afraid that just as Eve was deceived by the serpent's cunning, your minds may somehow be led astray from your sincere and pure devotion to Christ. For if someone comes to you and preaches a Jesus other than the Jesus we preached, or if you receive a different spirit from the one you received, or a different gospel from the one you accepted, *you put up with it easily enough*.
>
> 2 Corinthians 11:3-4, italics added

When we believe in the foolishness of the world, we are effectively rejecting the sufficiency of the Word.

"See to it that no one takes you captive through hollow and deceptive philosophy, which depends on human tradition and the basic principles of this world rather than on Christ."

Colossians 2:8

False teachings, myths, and opposing ideas have always been, and will always be, a part of the church. This fact, however, is not nearly as disturbing as the lack of awareness, concern, and rejection of these falsehoods within the body of Christ in the present day. How did it get this way? Simply put, we have put up with it too easily and for too long!

Because forgiveness is so essential to individual Christians, to God, to life, and to the body of Christ, it makes perfect sense that Satan will do everything possible to undermine this vital truth. While many look for the glaring and obvious attempts (and there are many) to destroy the truth concerning mercy and grace, the more effective lies will always be the more subtle distortions.

These deadly lies are like computer viruses. Have you ever had something pop up on your computer screen that says, "If you would like to download a virus that will cause your hard drive to crash so that you will lose everything on your computer, please click Yes"? Why don't you ever see such a blatant attempt? Because no one (well okay, *almost* no one) would fall for it.

The most effective and, therefore, the most destructive viruses are the ones you never see and where you are somehow duped into allowing them in. This is why it's wise to constantly be up-to-date with your anti-virus software. In the same way, we need to be up to speed with God's Word, so that we can easily discern, detect, and destroy the popular "viruses" which the world so cleverly puts forward.

Today, the gospel is often packaged and marketed (think Trojan horse) by such cunning themes, partial truths, and outright lies as:

- One hundred and one (insert any number!) easy secrets to happiness and fulfillment.

- Improve your self-worth…come to Jesus.

- Learn how to get others to fill your love tank.

- Come to Jesus, and you will get all the things that you have always wanted in life.

- Your biggest problem is low self-esteem. But "the good news" is that Christ died to give you high self-esteem.

- Name it and claim it. It is your *right* to have it.

- All your prayers will be answered the way you want them to be answered.

- You can get all that you want in this life.

- You *deserve* love and blessings.

- Come to our church and you will never struggle, never worry, never have health problems, never experience financial difficulties, never have trouble in relationships, always receive the respect that you "deserve," not to mention that you will find the perfect spouse, have perfect kids, and enjoy a fulfilling, high- paying career.

Imagine what Paul, Peter, John, or even Jesus could have done if they had only had a good marketing plan! Chances are that you and/or someone you know has fallen for one or more of the above subtle lies.

All of these themes have one main function: to quietly draw our attention away from the abundant sufficiency of God and His Word. This shrewd tactic coerces us into putting our hope in the world and in people—anything outside of God. "Let him not deceive himself by trusting in what is *worthless*" (Job 15:31, italics added).

With this misplaced hope we are primed to fail. Moreover, when we fail we usually go looking for help back at the same broken source of our failure. This vicious cycle must be a sampling of what hell will be like: repeatedly putting your hope into what is hopeless (Jer 17:5-6, 9; Is 55:1-2; Rom 1:25; 1 Cor 1:18-25).

> My people have committed two sins: They have forsaken me, the spring of living water, and have dug their own cisterns, broken cisterns that cannot hold water.
>
> Jeremiah 2:13

This way of life—repeatedly doing the same thing over and over and expecting different results—is the definition of insanity for many. "The hearts of men, moreover, are full of evil and *there is madness in their hearts* while they live" (Ecc 9:3, italics added).

The sad reality is that some of us have mistakenly, naively, or even overtly signed up for an altered form of Christianity. It may not be as obvious as some transparently fake gospels, but it is subtly off the mark just enough to keep us away from the truth.

When we live our lives by this misinformation, it is no wonder that we struggle to make sense of the terrible treatment we receive from others, including our fellow brothers and sisters in Christ. These lies and half-truths will also surely blind us to the ensuing need for, and beauty of, forgiveness.

How many of us are shocked and dismayed when God allows some difficult trial into our lives? How many of us believe God is love, that He is good, faithful, etc., *in theory*, even teaching these things to others; yet, inwardly we struggle to believe and experience this as actual reality? How many of us lack joy? Peace? Hope? Abundant life? How many of us are frequently disappointed, angry, worried, depressed, and bitter?

When this is the case, more often than not, our problem is that we inwardly believe in a worldly "gospel," one that says we can and will find our life here on earth. We fall for this subtle, but effective, propaganda even in the face of Jesus' continual exhortation to lose our

When we fail we usually go looking for help back at the same broken source of our failure.

How many of us lack joy...peace ...hope... abundant life?

This is usually because we inwardly believe In a worldly "gospel," one that says we can and will find our life here on earth.

lives, to deny ourselves, to serve others, to pick up our crosses daily, to walk in His steps, and to no longer live for ourselves.

However covert the errors in it, if we assent to this bogus gospel, we are pursuing the exact opposite of Jesus' desire. By believing these distortions of the truth: our hope is in this world, not in Him; we believe our goal is to perfect our *circumstances* so that we can achieve *happiness*; we walk by sight and not by faith; we are attempting to lay up treasure on earth, not in heaven; our eyes are fixed on what is seen and, therefore, what is temporary; we fear man and, because of this, are limited to, and controlled by, the thoughts and actions of others. This is misery. This is the absence of life, which is *death*.

How many of the people mentioned in the eleventh chapter of Hebrews, especially in verses thirty-five through thirty-eight, seem to have been concerned with fairness, rights, respect, felt-needs, emotional needs, self-worth, self-esteem, self-image, having their "love-tank" filled, secrets to happiness, a satisfying career, what others thought of them, or being rewarded on earth? In stark contrast, how many of them are commended simply and *solely* for their faith in God?

Yet, if you were to go to your local Christian bookstore, you would find between fifty to eighty percent of the books for sale there to be full of the preceding falsehoods. No wonder we struggle to forgive. No wonder we struggle to know God and the sufficiency of His Word, love, and provision. We are surrounded on all sides, including the *inside*, with the false teachings of the world.

> We are surrounded on all sides, including the inside, with the false teachings of the world.

Having looked at Hebrews 11 with its "heroes of faith," the next chapter of Hebrews speaks to each of us, as Christians, regarding our life here on earth. Take a moment now to read Hebrews 12, and look for the answers to the following questions:

- What are we to focus on?

- Does our encouragement come from getting what we want (even answered prayer)?

- Who, ultimately, is behind hardship and discipline?

- What are the purposes of suffering?

- How essential is forgiveness?

- How deadly is unforgiveness?

- Is our hope in this life?

- Is it happiness or holiness we are to pursue?

- Are we to live for the moment and/or what is temporary (as Esau did), or for God's grand agenda?

> When we pursue the world's goals, we are essentially despising God's glory, His blessings, and His love.

- Are we to come to Jesus, or seek to find our selves?

- Is our hope in that which can be shaken (the creation/man),
  or does God want to remove these things so that we cannot be shaken?

Esau's story is a prime illustration of the absurdity of temporary fulfillment in the context of God's supreme desire (see Gen 25:27-34). Is it wrong to eat a bowl of lentil stew? Not necessarily. But, is it a horrific blunder, even the height of foolishness and godlessness, to give up your birthright to incredible responsibility and blessing, all for a single meal (Heb 12:16-17)? Likewise, when we pursue the world's goals, we are essentially despising God's glory, blessings, and love.

"The unfolding of your words gives light" (Ps 119:130). With just a chapter or two from God's Word, we have exposed the falsehoods, worldly wisdom, and godless myths which the majority of today's popular Christian books contain, at least in part. The reality is that if we were to be true to God and His Word, using the Bible as our solid standard, we would need to remove the label of "Christian" from at least half of the literature being peddled as such.

Even so, what does all of this have to do with forgiveness? Everything! If your understanding of God and His purposes in your life is erroneous, then how will you grasp and appreciate the realities of this life? How off the mark will your expectations be? What kind of God will you come to know? What will you be thankful for? Why will you worship, praise, and love God? How will you handle life's difficulties and your mistreatment at the hands of others?

Buying into a gospel tainted by man's wisdom will slowly but surely draw you away from truth, God's love, God's character, God's purposes for your life, and God's perfect and life-giving grace and mercy. The bottom line is that we can either buy into and follow a gospel that, at its heart, has *me* and *my happiness* as its purpose and passion (man-centered), or we can choose to believe in the gospel where *God* is everything! (See Ps 16:11, 23, 27:4, 62:5-7, 63:2-5, 84:10, 130:7; Is 58:11; Jer 17:8; Zeph 3:17; Mk 12:30; Lk 10:42; 1 Cor 10:31; Phil 3:7-9; Col 3:17, 3:23; 2 Tim 3:15-17; 2 Pet 1:3-4.)

The true gospel ceaselessly opposes one's flesh, and is offensive to the world's wisdom and desires. How foolish it is to believe that we can take the perpetually corrupt, yet always popular, ideas, philosophy, and cravings of the world and somehow harmonize it with God's pure, perfect, and sufficient Word. Yet, there is no shortage of Christians who attempt to do just that. Not surprisingly, their books sell by the thousands year after year.

Instead of slickly packaged appeals to our flesh, it is *Jesus* who is the gospel's sole attraction, and it is He who should be enthusiastically pursued and delightfully enjoyed with all of our heart, soul, mind, and strength, all the days of our lives. "*You* have made known to me the path of life; *you* will fill me with joy in your presence, with eternal pleasures at *your* right hand" (Ps 16:11, italics added).

Not only should God be our exclusive objective, but His glory and kingdom usually come at the expense of our fair treatment, self-esteem, "wisdom," self-worth, strength, "emotional needs," happiness, pride, success, etc. (Lk 9:23-24; Jn 12:25; 2 Cor 1:8-9, 5:15; Phil 2:5-11, 3:7-11; Heb 12:10-11). And without this understanding, we will struggle mightily with forgiveness, anger, love, and life.

Every bogus gospel will appeal powerfully to our lusts and fit easily into our fleshly mode of operation. Our sinful nature's attention and energy are eagerly given to pathetic attempts to control and/or change situations and people (rather than changing our hearts) for the sole purpose of achieving our own happiness, comfort, and self-gratification. All of this "spoiled food" (Jn 6:27) and fleeting pleasure comes at the expense of seeking God first and foremost, along with His kingdom, His purposes, and His glory.

Every bogus gospel will appeal powerfully to our lusts and fit easily into our fleshly mode of operation.

The thinking and "logic" of the worldly gospel is along the lines of, "If I just had _____ , then I would be happy. Therefore, I absolutely NEED _____ " (see Satan's subtle message to Eve; Gen 3:1-5). This "gospel" usually combines some truth with a normal desire and puffs it up with distortion and deception until it is an absolute "I have to have it now" *need* (see Esau; Heb 12:16-17). Hence, the popularity of the "needs" gospel. "If only I was married…." "If only I made more money I could…" "I need alcohol to deal with…" "If I was better looking (e.g., weighed less, looked younger, had more muscles, had plastic surgery) then…" "If only I had higher self-esteem then…" "If only my spouse met my emotional needs, then…"

These desires and pursuits (or "needs") become nothing less than idols in our hearts (Ezek 14:1-5, 20:16; Is 44:1-20) that control us and draw us away from God. Whatever we "need" controls us. What is more, such idols make us worthless… "They followed worthless idols and themselves became worthless" (1 Ki 17:15).

Whatever you "need" controls you.

Every bogus gospel will always turn God's design and desire upside down (Is 29:13-16, 5:20; Rom 1:25). The real gospel teaches that through God's wisdom, love, and sovereignty, all the circumstances and people (good and bad) that one encounters are divinely interwoven into his life. They are put there, not so much to be controlled or manipulated, but as opportunities to be faithful to God, to trust His Word, to please Him, to imitate Him, to worship Him, to love Him, and to glorify Him as one learns to love others and to conform to the image of Christ.

"But what about me?" "Doesn't God want me to be happy?" "Does God not love me or want to bless me?" The reality is that God often intentionally sacrifices our happiness and perceived "needs" for the far greater good. We need to trust God IF, when, or how He wants to bless us—even if, and especially when, the blessing comes in the form of suffering (Job 2:10; Ps 119:71, 119:75; Jer 29:11-14; Rom 5:3-5; 2 Cor 12:9-10; Jas 1:2-4; 1 Pet 1:6-9).

The reality is that God often intentionally sacrifices our happiness and perceived "needs" for the far greater good.

Again, our hope is not in our circumstances, in people, or in the pursuit of happiness, but solely in the character of God (love, goodness, faithfulness, power, provision, wisdom, etc.). To the extent that we are faithful to His message, promises, design, and character (i.e., love for God; 1 Jn 5:3), we will experience love, power, fullness, hope, growth, joy, peace, patience, etc.

When God is glorified we, as a result, are blessed beyond comprehension.

I pray that out of his glorious riches he may strengthen you with power through his Spirit in your inner being, so that Christ may dwell in your hearts through faith. And I pray that you, being rooted and established in love, may have power, together with all the saints, to grasp how wide and long and high and deep is the love of Christ, and to know this love that surpasses knowledge—that you may be filled to the measure of all the fullness of God. Now to him who is able to do immeasurably more than we all ask or imagine, according to his power that is at work within us, to him be glory in the church and in Christ Jesus throughout all generations, for ever and ever! Amen.

Ephesians 3:16-21

"Yeah, but…can I trust God's character?" Paul overwhelmingly satisfies this concern in a single verse with the powerful and divine logic of proven sacrificial love.

He who did not spare his own Son, but gave him up for us all–how will he not also, along with him, graciously give us all things?

Romans 8:32

Remember, every bogus gospel will teach subtly, if not overtly, that "God is not enough," that "you *need* _____ ," in addition to God, and that your hope is in this world and in the performance of man (Jer 2:13; Rom 1:25).

Hopefully, we will easily see the obvious falsehoods; but, we need to also beware of the more subtle "fine sounding arguments" (Col 2:4), "godless chatter" (1 Tim 6:20), and "godless myths" (1 Tim 4:7) that "suit their own desires" (2 Tim 4:3). No matter what happens, our hope must always be in "God *ALONE*" (Ps 62, 73:23-28; Rom 1:25, 15:13; 1 Tim 5:5-6; 1 Pet 1:13; 2 Pet 1:3-4).

If our infinite, all-loving, all-powerful, eternal, gracious, all-knowing, just, merciful, compassionate, forgiving, perfect God who loves us, pours out His love into our hearts, and dwells in us is not enough, then who or what will make up for His perceived lack? Man? His "wisdom"? The world? Its "wisdom"?

Timothy, guard what has been entrusted to your care. *Turn away from godless chatter and the opposing ideas of what is falsely called knowledge,* which some have professed and in so doing have wandered from the faith.

1 Timothy 6:20-21, italics added

We must pay more careful attention, therefore, to what we have heard, so that we do not drift away.

Hebrews 2:1

Watch your life and doctrine closely. Persevere in them, because if you do, you will save both yourself and your hearers.

1 Timothy 4:16

> Every bogus gospel will teach subtly, if not overtly, that "God is not enough."
>
> Who or what will make up for God's perceived lack?

- On a scale of zero to ten, with ten being a mountain and zero being a molehill, how would you rate this area as a stumbling block to your forgiveness of others?

- Why?

26

Stumbling Blocks To Forgiveness: # 9

"Yeah, but..."

One of the most common stumbling blocks to forgiveness is that we are plagued with a serious and deadly heart condition—referred to here as the "Yeah, But..." Disorder ("YBD"). Our failure to forgive often boils down to a stubborn, rebellious, ungrateful, and prideful *refusal* to forgive.

The ugliest and darkest part of our heart is exposed when we *know* the right way, God's way, and yet remain stubbornly unwilling to submit our warped will to God's perfect will. This is madness! This is death! This is the ultimate slap in the face to God, if that were possible. This is knowing the truth but constantly looking for and inserting our own convenient loopholes and escape clauses into God's perfect and beautiful design, all in a feeble attempt to fulfill our corrupt desires.

Much of this heart condition has already been described, yet at least two chief components go into this fatal syndrome. First, we have ungrateful hearts.

> But mark this: There will be *terrible* times in the last days. People will be *lovers of themselves*, lovers of money, boastful, proud, abusive, disobedient to their parents, *ungrateful*, unholy, *without love, unforgiving*, slanderous, without self-control, brutal, not lovers of the good, treacherous, rash, conceited, *lovers of pleasure rather than lovers of God--*having a form of godliness but denying its power. Have nothing to do with them.
>
> 2 Timothy 3:1-5, italics added

> Let the peace of Christ rule in your hearts, since as members of one body you were called to peace. And *be thankful*. Let the word of Christ dwell in you richly as you teach and admonish one another with all wisdom, and as you sing psalms, hymns and spiritual songs *with gratitude in your*

YBD:

"Yeah But Disorder"

This is the ultimate slap in the face to God.

hearts to God. And whatever you do, whether in word or deed, do it all in the name of the Lord Jesus, *giving thanks to God the Father through him.*

Colossians 3:15-17, italics added

"*Yeah*, God gave me grace and mercy when I deserved death, hell, and eternal torment, *but* that person hurt me too much for me to forgive him."

We do not come close to fully grasping and appreciating the enormity and cost of our own sinfulness. This cheapens Jesus' love, glory, death, resurrection, grace, mercy, and gift of life. In addition, this tends to make us a lot more important than we really are (see *Chapter 25* regarding the concepts of "self-esteem," "self-worth," and "bogus gospel"). Therefore, we struggle to be grateful for God's unimaginable and undeserved Gift that He graciously gave us. If we were truly grateful, then we would forgive anyone and anything.

> He seldom reflects on the days of his life, because *God keeps him occupied with gladness of heart.*

Ecclesiastes 5:20, italics added

Along with an ungrateful heart, the second major component of YBD is that we simply *refuse to forgive.* By taking such a position, a stubborn and prideful heart (literally "full of pride") is revealed—one that is severely lacking in fear of, and love for, God.

> But *because of your stubbornness and your unrepentant heart*, you are storing up wrath against yourself for the day of God's wrath, when his righteous judgment will be revealed. God "will give to each person according to what he has done." To those who by persistence in doing good seek glory, honor and immortality, he will give eternal life. But for those who are *self-seeking* and who *reject the truth* and *follow evil*, there will be wrath and anger. There will be trouble and distress for every human being who does evil: first for the Jew, then for the Gentile; but glory, honor and peace for everyone who does good: first for the Jew, then for the Gentile.

Romans 2:5-10, italics added

> But these people have stubborn and rebellious hearts; they have turned aside and gone away. They do not say to themselves, "Let us fear the Lord our God, who gives autumn and spring rains in season, who assures us of the regular weeks of harvest." Your wrongdoings have kept these away; your sins have deprived you of good.

Jeremiah 5:23-25

> But they did not listen or pay attention; *instead, they followed the stubborn inclinations of their evil hearts.* **They went backward and not forward.**

Jeremiah 7:24, italics added

If we were truly grateful, then we would forgive anyone and anything.

"They went backward and not forward."

Jeremiah 7:24

"*Yeah*, I know I am required to forgive, *but* they are the ones that hurt me. They need to come to me and make up for all the pain they caused me." "*Yeah, but* they started it!"

Such a stance is nothing less than rebellion. It is essentially spitting in the face of God. This may sound harsh, but if we know what it is that God desires and commands us to do, if we know how to do it, if we know that God cherishes forgiveness, if we know that forgiveness is best for everyone involved, if we know that only Satan wins through our unforgiveness, and we *still* refuse to forgive, then it becomes a personal affront to God.

Our pride and rebellion must be exceptionally mind-boggling to God, in light of the fact that instead of the wrath that we deserve, He has given us mercy, grace, love, and eternal life. This stumbling block is closely related to, and influenced by, the ungrateful and unchanged heart.

When we choose to rebel in this way, we are living for the deadly lie of pride (my rights, my goodness, my worth, my esteem, my ability, my will, my fair share, my vengeance, my happiness) while refusing to humble ourselves for the benefit of all (except Satan) and the glory of God. This is a matter of your will versus God's will. Who wins in this encounter? Who always, always, always loses in this particular "battle of the wills"?

By pursuing the desires of our flesh, we will avoid and even loathe God and His Word. We will crave the "feel good" false teachings of the world much more than the truth (2 Tim 4:3-4). In this state of mind, anyone who teaches or confronts us with God's Word will also be despised and even attacked.

> These are rebellious people, deceitful children, children unwilling to listen to the Lord's instruction. They say to the seers, "See no more visions!" and to the prophets, "*Give us no more visions of what is right! Tell us pleasant things, prophesy illusions.* Leave this way, get off this path, and *stop confronting us with the Holy One of Israel!*"
>
> Isaiah 30:9-11, italics added

This was part of Jeremiah's experience in confronting Israel's stubbornness with God's truth:

> But they will reply, "It's no use. We will continue with our own plans; *each of us will follow the stubbornness of his evil heart*...So come, *let's attack him with our tongues and pay no attention to anything he says.*"
>
> Jeremiah 18:12, 18, italics added

What does God say to the stubborn? How will He treat those who still refuse to follow His design and desire? Consider His warning to Israel:

> If after all this you will not listen to Me, I will punish you for your sins seven times over. *I will break down your stubborn pride* and make the sky above you like iron and the ground beneath you like bronze. Your strength will be spent in vain, because your soil will not yield its crops, nor

YBD:
A matter of your will versus God's will.

will the trees of the land yield their fruit. If you remain hostile toward Me and refuse to listen to Me, I will multiply your afflictions seven times over, *as your sins deserve.*

Leviticus 26:18-21, italics added

The stubborn unwillingness of an unyielding heart is the flesh's last line of defense against forgiveness, freedom, and life. Once this stronghold is breeched, however, all sorts of love, joy, mercy, peace, hope, grace, power, and blessings come flooding in.

The one essential weapon for this victory is *humility* (note: the opposite of what the world teaches). "Humble yourselves before the Lord, and He will lift you up" (Jas 4:10). Get rid of your pride. Put God, others, and His desires above yourself (Phil 2:1-8). You need to lose your life so that you can find it (Lk 9:23-24). You need to be crucified with Christ (Gal 2:20; Col 3:3). You must stop living for yourself and start living for God (2 Cor 5:15).

Although easier said than done, you simply need to change your "Yeah, but…" into "Yes, Lord!" You need to desire, believe, and act upon the loving and trusting attitude of Christ…"Not my will, but your will be done" (Lk 22:42).

God opposes the proud but gives grace to the humble.

James 4:6

This is what the LORD says:
"Stand at the crossroads and look;
ask for the ancient paths,
ask where the good way is, and walk in it,
and you will find rest for your souls.
But you said, 'We will not walk in it.'

Jeremiah 6:16, italics added

> The stubborn unwillingness of an unyielding heart is the flesh's last line of defense against forgiveness, freedom, and life.

- On a scale of zero to ten, with ten being a mountain and zero being a molehill, how would you rate this area as a stumbling block to your forgiveness of others?

- Why?

- Add up your numbers from the previous scales in *Chapters 18-26, "Stumbling Blocks To Forgiveness."* Write the total here:

- What does this number reveal to you?

- Which of the previous stumbling blocks do you struggle with the most? Why do you think this is?

• What do you need to do to change and grow in this area?

 All of these issues repeatedly point to our desperate need to change our hearts. It is of utmost importance that our hearts become more like Jesus' heart (Matt 18:35; Lk 23:34; Acts 7:60; Rom 8:28-29; 2 Cor 3:18; Eph 5:1-2, 6:6-7).

God's merciful, life-giving gift should not just save us from hell, it should also radically transform our hearts each and every day. If God's love does not make you a different person, than something is terribly wrong. Like the church at Ephesus, your problem and your sin is that "You have forsaken your first love" (Rev 2:4). If so, you need to go back to where you began and, as Scripture says, "Remember the height from which you have fallen! Repent and do the things you did at first" (Rev 2:5).

Nehemiah described five beautiful characteristics of God: "But you are a *forgiving* God, *gracious* and *compassionate, slow to anger* and *abounding in love*" (Neh 9:17, italics added). We need to "imitate" Christ (Eph 4:32-5:2) in this same manner...forgiving, gracious, compassionate, slow to anger, and, most importantly, abounding in love (first, knowing God's love, and then freely overflowing with this same love; 1 Jn 4:16). How different would your life be if these characteristics were true of you?

Growing in these areas of potential stumbling blocks will not only help you to forgive others, it will radically transform everything about you. On the other hand, failure to grow in these areas will definitely cause you to move further and further away from God; in addition you will continue to experience more and more fruit of destruction in your life (e.g., bitterness, despair, worry, fear, depression, and strained, painful, destructive relationships).

27

WHAT IS SO AMAZING?

Amazing grace! How sweet the sound,
That saved a wretch like me!
I once was lost, but now am found;
Was blind, but now I see.

'Twas grace that taught my heart to fear,
And grace my fears relieved;
How precious did that grace appear
The hour I first believed.

Through many dangers, toils and snares,
I have already come;
'Tis grace hath brought me safe thus far,
And grace will lead me home.

The Lord has promised good to me,
His Word my hope secures;
He will my Shield and Portion be,
As long as life endures.

Yea, when this flesh and heart shall fail,
And mortal life shall cease,
I shall possess, within the veil,
A life of joy and peace.

The earth shall soon dissolve like snow,
The sun forbear to shine;
But God, Who called me here below,
Shall be forever mine.

When we've been there ten thousand years,
Bright shining as the sun,
We've no less days to sing God's praise
Than when we'd first begun.

John Newton

- Why was grace (forgiveness) so amazing and sweet-sounding to the hymn writer?

 Was it not because he was fully and painfully aware of who he was: a lost, blind "wretch"? If you think about it, John Newton was little different from you and me.

- Do you gladly sing the phrase "a wretch like me"? Why or why not?

- How does your experience with grace compare (e.g., "amazing," "sweet," "precious," or so-so, don't understand it, don't appreciate it)?

28 FORGIVENESS QUESTIONS

The following specifics are helpful reminders when we find ourselves asking the "who, what, when, where, how, and why" questions in regard to forgiveness.

Who to forgive:

- **EVERYONE**
  We are to forgive *every* person who offends or hurts us (Matt 6:12, 6:14-15; Mk 11:25; Col 3:13). Sorry, no exceptions!

What to forgive:

- **EVERYTHING**
  We are to forgive *every* thing that is done against us (Mk 11:25; Eph 4:31-32). This includes the big things and the little things (1 Pet 4:8; Prov 10:12). Often, the little irritations accumulate to become a formidable foe. Before you know it, resentment inhabits your heart. On the other hand, when we freely and continually forgive from a gracious and loving heart, we will easily "cover over" these offenses.

> We have no right to hold anything against anyone, ever.

When to forgive:

- **CONTINUOUSLY**
  We are to forgive *continuously* (Matt 18:21-22; Lk 17:4; Jn 15:12-13; Col 3:12-13), out of a heart full of gratitude and thanksgiving, characterized by grace, mercy, and love.

- **ALWAYS**
  We are to *always* forgive—and as soon as possible. Forgiveness is not dependent, per se, on the contrition, confession, repentance, or request of the offender, but on God's love and forgiveness of you. His command and desire is for you to do the same, resulting in the transformation of your character. It is always ideal for the offender to seek forgiveness, but, sadly, this does not

happen nearly enough. Either way, we have no right to hold anything against anyone, ever (Matt 6:12, 14-15; Mk 11:25; Lk 6:37; Col 3:13).

Where to forgive:

- **EVERYWHERE**
  We are called to practice forgiveness *wherever* we come into contact with other fellow sinners (Matt 10:8, 18:35; Lk 7:47; Eph 4:32-5:2; Col 3:12-17). This means in *every* relationship you have. Again, there are no exceptions.

How to forgive:

- **REMEMBER**
  First and foremost, we must remember the grace and forgiveness that we have received. This knowledge will enable us to forgive others out of an abundantly loved, loving, forgiven, merciful, transformed and grateful heart.

- **CHOOSE**
  We must make the conscious choice, *out of love* (i.e., not treating a person according to what I judge he deserves), to not hold the debt of the offense against the offendor—to purposefully not give him what he deserves (i.e., mercy).

- **COMMIT**
  In order to truly effect forgiveness, we must make a *deep commitment* not to talk about the offense with either the offender or with anyone else (i.e., gossip), or to dwell on the offense/hurt again. When we are tempted to, we must instead meditate on the abundant and undeserved love and forgiveness we ourselves have been given by God.

- **PRAY**
  It is essential, and also highly beneficial, to *pray* for the offender (Matt 5:44-45; Lk 6:28) on a daily basis.

- **PRACTICE**
  We must continually *practice* forgiveness, rather than viewing it simply as a one-time event. Forgiveness is a process that lasts in proportion to the severity of the hurt. The deeper the hurt, the longer the forgiveness process takes.

> We are called to practice forgiveness wherever we come into contact with other fellow sinners.

> Forgiveness is a process that lasts in proportion to the severity of the hurt. The deeper the hurt, the longer the forgiveness process takes.

Why we forgive:

- **FOR THE GLORY OF GOD**
  "Whatever you do, do it all for the glory of God" (1 Cor 10:31b; see also 2 Cor 3:18; Col 3:17).

- **GOD COMMANDS IT**
  "Bear with each other and forgive whatever grievances you may have against one another. Forgive as the Lord forgave you" (Col 3:13; see also Matt 6:12-15; Lk 17:3; Mk 11:25; Eph 4:31-32).

- **GOD FORGAVE US**
  "When the kindness and love of God our Savior appeared, He saved us, not because of righteous things we had done, but because of His mercy" (Ti 3:4-5; see also Matt 18:21-35; Rom 5:8; Eph 4:30-32; Col 3:13).

- **TO LOVE GOD**
  "Love the Lord your God with all your heart and with all your soul and with all your mind and with all your strength" (Mk 12:30; see also 1 Jn 4:16-17).

- **TO LOVE OTHERS**
  "A new command I give you: Love one another. As I have loved you, so you must love one another" (Jn 13:34; see also Jn 15:12-13; Mk 12:31).

- **FOR THE BENEFIT OF OTHERS**
  "See to it that no one misses the grace of God and that no bitter root grows up to cause trouble and defile many" (Heb 12:15; see also 2 Cor 2:5-11).

- **FOR OUR OWN BENEFIT**
  "Blessed are the merciful, for they will be shown mercy" (Matt 5:7; see also Job 5:2; Matt 18:33-35; Mk 11:25; Gal 5:1).

"Forgive as the Lord forgave you."

Colossians 3:13

"See to it that no one misses the grace of God."

Hebrews 12:15

"To this you were called."

1 Peter 3:9

- Why, specifically, do you struggle to forgive? *(See "Stumbling Blocks To Forgiveness," Chapters 18-26.)*

- Who in your life (past or present) would you say needs to be forgiven by you? List below all of the names of:

    1. Those people who do not deserve forgiveness.
    2. Those people whom you have not forgiven.
    3. Those people whom you resent or have bitterness toward.

(If necessary, for the sake of privacy, write names on a separate sheet of paper.)

 By specifically giving those who have hurt you mercy and grace, you will not only please God, you will also experience the blessings of freedom, joy, peace, and love, all while transforming your heart and life. Commit now, out of a grateful, forgiven, loving, merciful, and changing heart, to forgive all that these people have done to you (this includes the "What" that needs to be forgiven).

Write down the offenders' names (above), and pray for them on a daily basis. Pray that they will be blessed by God's grace and mercy. Pray that they will come to a deep knowledge of God, truth, and repentance. Pray that they too will become free. Entrust them entirely to God.

"Do not repay evil with evil or insult with insult, but with blessing, because *to this you were called* so that you may inherit a blessing" (1 Pet 3:9, italics added).

"If your enemy is hungry, feed him; if he is thirsty, give him something to drink. In doing this, you will heap burning coals on his head. Do not be overcome by evil, but overcome evil with good" (Rom 12:20-21).

Whenever you are tempted to talk about or dwell on the past or current pain, remember and meditate on your own unmerited favor that you received from Christ and His death on the cross for you. God's indescribable gift, graciously and lovingly given to you, should continually be at the forefront of your mind. *The more His love and gift occupy your thoughts and heart, the harder it will be for you not to forgive.*

29

Often we are unaware of, and blind to, our own bitterness. Possibly the worst case scenario in life is a person who thinks that he has forgiven, but, in reality, has not. The following outward signs are probable indicators of an inward struggle and/or refusal to forgive. The more rampant this fruit in a person's life, the more likely that person is unforgiving and bitter. Some indicators are more obvious than others.

Check yourself for these signs first. Then ask several people who know you best and are willing to tell you the truth (your spouse, children, siblings, friends, etc.) if they think that you struggle with unforgiveness or any of its indicators.

Signs that you may not be truly forgiving others:

- **Unhappiness, Discontentment, Misery**
  You struggle with unhappiness, misery, and the ability to be content. Bitter people are simply not content; unforgiveness results in a torturous life.

- **Ungratefulness**
  You are not often thankful or you have a hard time giving thanks.

- **Addictions**
  You struggle with items that people sometimes become "addicted" to: e.g., alcohol, pornography, food, drugs, obtaining and/or spending money—essentially, seeking pleasure. (There is a strong correlation, in my experience, between "addictions" and unforgiveness or bitterness.)

- **Problems with Anger**
  You live life based on getting what you desire and fulfilling your "rights" according to what you deem most important…your *self*.

- **Performance-Based Life and Relationships**
  Your life is based on or driven by performance—that of both yourself and others. This is characterized by any or all of the following: perfectionism, high expectations and demands; self-righteousness; subscribing to the "needs" mindset; experiencing frequent disappointment, anger, worry, etc.

> Unforgiveness results in a tortuous life.

> There is a strong correlation between "addictions" and unforgiveness.

- **Depression, Despair**

  You struggle with depression and/or despair: the common results of continuously putting hope in what is broken, hopeless, and unfixable (see descriptions under *"Performance-Based," "Anger;" "Addictions,"* etc.).

- **Poor Examples**

  One or both of your parents struggled with bitterness, unforgiveness, or resentment (this is where we usually learn how to handle or *mishandle* life's difficulties).

- **Critical and Judgmental**

  You are not easily pleased. You easily find fault in others (heavily related to *"Unhappiness"* and *"Performance-Based"*).

- **Biting Words, Harsh Comments, Cutting Sarcasm**

  You are often sarcastic and cutting in your remarks to other people. Bitter people cut, stab, and bludgeon others with their words, their built-up bitterness coming through in what they say. Our words reflect our heart: "Out of the overflow of his heart his mouth speaks" (Lk 6:45). In contrast, loving and forgiving people find little use for the weapon of a sharp tongue (see *"Critical"*).

- **Poor Relationships**

  You have poor relationships for the most part. Unforgiveness leads to tenuous relationships, as well as a lack of good long-term relationships. People "walk on eggshells" around you. You, as well as others in your life, suffer from the ever-mounting pressure of unresolved conflict, while you either refuse and/or are unable to resolve conflict.

- **Insecurity**

  You are insecure—a sure indication that you have misplaced your hope, putting it in the performance of people and temporary circumstances. Because there is only one place to be truly secure—in God—if your hope is anywhere else, you will ultimately be insecure. This is an indication that your treasure and, therefore, your heart is in temporary things rather than the eternal. You are walking by sight, not by faith.

- **Loneliness**

  You are lonely, often in spite of an outward appearance to the contrary. This is sometimes the result of pushing others away with your demands for a desired performance on their part, as you put your hope in the hopeless performance of sinful man. Sadly, because you demand fulfillment from others, the usual result is that no one will want to be around you.

- **Me-Centeredness**

  Your focus is, more often than not, on yourself. Some indications that you are focused on yourself can be seen in such ways as: the majority of your conversations with others are about *you*; instead of truly listening to what someone else is saying, you are thinking about what *you* can say next—which is usually something about

> Do you easily find fault with others?

> Our words reflect our heart: loving and forgiving people find little use for the weapon of a sharp tongue.

> Have you misplaced your hope?

you; you are more concerned with how others are treating *you* than with how you are treating *others*; you expect and/or demand that other people meet your perceived "needs"; and when you do give, it's usually in order to get something back. This is the wisdom of the world and the desire of your flesh at work together: e.g., the concepts of high self-esteem, self-worth, self-image, and self-love. However, in direct opposition to these ideas, James writes that "disorder and *every evil practice*" come from *selfish ambition* (Jas 3:16, italics added). In addition, the more focused you are on yourself, the less you are focused on God and others. This is the *antithesis of love* because love "is not self-seeking" (1 Cor. 13:5).

Are you more concerned with how others are treating you or with how you are treating others?

- **Constant Drama**
  Your life is characterized by "drama," whether real or perceived. You could be referred to as a "drama queen/king" or a "high maintenance personality" because you somehow always find yourself in the midst of a crisis or offense. In addition, you drain those around you with constant unresolved problems or worries. Furthermore, you usually see yourself as the victim, no matter what the situation— it's always someone else's fault. Overall, you lack peace and contentment.

- **Overdeveloped Sense of Fairness**
  Your life is measured mainly in terms of the "Fairness Doctrine." You frequently think or say, "that's not fair!" You have near-constant anger, frustration, and bitterness over injustices in life. Essentially, you are not living and walking in the New Covenant.

- **Fearful and Worried**
  You are overly concerned, even fearful, of how others will treat you. You could be termed a "people pleaser," as you constantly try to control that which you cannot control. You lack faith in God's perfect character, which results in a lack of love for God and others.

Do you frequently think or say, "that's not fair"?

- **Easily Hurt**
  You are easily hurt. This is related to the performance-based way of life: putting too much hope and expectations in sinful people. The more hope you put in people, rather than in God, the more easily hurt you will be.

- **Controlled by Emotions**
  You are very emotional and "moody." Your state of mind is heavily dependent upon circumstances and the performance of others rather than on God. Therefore, only if you are treated well and/or circumstances are good will you be "happy"; if people or circumstances treat you badly, you are overly sad and/or angry. The other extreme in this case is that you have difficulty showing any emotion whatsoever.

The more hope you put in people, rather than in God, the more easily hurt you will be.

- **Paranoid**
  You experience paranoia and other bizarre behavior patterns, including "conspiracy theories" usually centered around yourself. Again, the continual focus is on you and not on your true calling to love God and others. This behavior will eventually expose the "madness" in your heart; (Eccl. 9:3; see also Prov 28:1;

Ps 73:21-22), as you perpetually hope in that which continuously fails you: yourself, others, and circumstances.

- **Rebellious**
  You have difficulty submitting to anything, and you regularly display it by rebelling against most authority, although it has been placed in your life by God for a reason. You may occasionally submit outwardly, but you remain defiant inwardly.

- **Stubborn**
  You suffer from YBD ("Yeah, But Disorder" –see *Chapter 26*).

- **Stunted Growth**
  Overall, you lack growth, change, and maturity in your Christian walk.

- **Distance from God**
  Your relationship with God is distant, and not what it can and should be (see Matt 6:14-15).

In addition to the signs previously listed, the following three things are the most obvious indicators that you may not be truly forgiving others:

- **If you lack in knowing and/or giving love**
- **If you lack peace and joy, as well as the other fruit of the Spirit**
- **If you lack the experience of grace and mercy**

In contrast, the following are sure signs that you *do* experience grace and mercy:

- **The fruit of the Spirit**
- **Gratefulness**
- **Hope**
- **Freedom to enjoy life and others no matter what might happen**
- **Security**
- **Love**
- **A growing, mature, and strong relationship with God**

Do you perpetually hope in that which continuously fails you: your self, others, and circumstances?

Is your relationship with God distant, and not what it can and should be?

- Which of the signs, or fruit, of unforgiveness apply to you?

- Which signs do you think *other people* would say apply to you?

- What is revealed about the condition of your heart by your answers to the questions above?

30

THE PERFECT PLACE TO START

Come to me, all you who are weary and burdened, and I will give you rest. Take my yoke upon you and learn from me, for I am gentle and humble in heart, and you will find rest for your souls. For my yoke is easy and my burden is light.

Matthew 11:28-30

It is for freedom that Christ has set us free. Stand firm, then, and do not let yourselves be burdened again by a yoke of slavery.

Galatians 5:1

Therefore, since we are surrounded by such a great cloud of witnesses, let us throw off everything that hinders and the sin that so easily entangles, and let us run with perseverance the race marked out for us.

Hebrews 12:1

If you have bitterness in your heart, then you must be weary from its unbearable burden. The more you carry the weight of the past and the stress of its pain the more you will be worn out and miserable.

Jesus freely offers relief. He offers a new way. He graciously offers a new heart. He offers rest, strength, freedom, and abundant life. His gifts are precisely what the weary need and desire.

In spite of this, many complain that His way is too difficult. But, as we have seen, God's way may be more challenging at first, but His desire and design is infinitely easier than our old patterns. Is depression easier than joy? Are fear and worry easier than love and peace?

Still, many protest that it is too difficult to change their ways. The undeniable reality is that change *is* hard. But our life's experience is far more confined, problematic, and painful when we choose not to be transformed. Are perpetual torture and imprisonment easier than giving up our pride, stubbornness, and "rights"? Is living for vengeance easier than re-living grace, mercy, and love? Is fighting to save your life so that you will lose it easier than losing your life so that you will find life?

> Our life's experience is far more confined, problematic, and painful when we choose not to be transformed.

It is completely natural for us to have unforgiving hearts. Even if one grows up in entirely forgiving surroundings, it is conceivable that he could still become a bitter person. "An evil man is snared by his own sin" (Prov 29:6). Yet, be that as it may, we still need to acknowledge and deal with the outside influences upon our hearts.

> Do not make friends with a hot-tempered man,
> do not associate with one easily angered,
> or you may learn his ways
> and get yourself ensnared.
>
> Proverbs 22:24-25

We cannot choose our family, yet they are usually the biggest influence in our lives. Generally speaking, to the extent that our parents are wise, their wisdom will likely be instilled in us. In the same way, the foolishness of mom and/or dad will most likely impact our hearts and behavior.

> He who walks with the wise grows wise,
> but a companion of fools suffers harm.
>
> Proverbs 13:20

We all learn (good and bad) from what was modeled by our parents. Unfortunately, many people grow up in homes where forgiveness is absent. Grace and mercy are often misunderstood, poorly modeled, rarely practiced, and sometimes even outright despised and rejected. While we are always one hundred percent responsible for our choices, bitter people usually come from bitter families.

> See to it that no one misses the grace of God and that no bitter root grows
> up to cause trouble and defile many.
>
> Hebrews 12:15

Do not be misled: "Bad company corrupts good character."

> 1 Corinthians 15:33

It is important to remember that we are always responsible for our own behavior. While others, including family members, have a very real influence on us, we can never blame another person for our sin and sinful ways.

> *The soul who sins is the one who will die.* The son will not share the guilt of
> the father, nor will the father share the guilt of the son. The righteousness
> of the righteous man will be credited to him, and the wickedness of the
> wicked will be charged against him.
>
> Ezekiel 19:20, italics added

If a person comes from a bitter home, then it is highly likely that one or both of his parents came from a bitter family as well. If this is true, then it is also highly probable that the parents' parents came from painful and unforgiving environments as well. This dreadful pattern may go back several generations. While this does not alleviate any individual's

Is living for vengeance easier than re-living grace, mercy, and love?

Bitter people usually come from bitter families.

"See to it that no one misses the grace of God and that no bitter root grows up to cause trouble and defile many."

Hebrews 12:15

A Beautiful Life

responsibility, it can provide much-needed compassion in order for us to appreciate what others have gone through. It helps us understand what is perhaps *behind* what a person does.

You need not repeat any bittern pattern that exists in your family. Instead of re-living your parents' pain, why not learn and grow from their trouble and grief? Understanding, forgiving, and loving your parents, no matter what you may think they deserve, will go a long way in freeing you from much potential anguish.

You need not repeat any bittern pattern that exists in your family.

A dysfunctional family is an unforgiving family. Those who belong to such families tend to lack the functional belief, desire, know-how, and behavior of mercy and grace (a.k.a. love). And, as we have noted, an unforgiving family tends to beget more unforgiving families. However, all is not lost if you or someone you know grew up stained by these surroundings.

> Because of the Lord's great love we are not consumed,
> for his compassions never fail.
> *They are new every morning;*
> great is your faithfulness.
>
> Lamentations 3:22-23, italics added

Your life and especially your family does not have to be defiled with the poison of bitterness. You can break the cycle. You can start over. You can have a new beginning. But you need to take responsibility for *your* behavior. You need to humble yourself, confess, repent, and seek forgiveness for your sin, especially your own bitterness and the impact it has had on those around you.

"His compassions never fail. They are new every morning."

Lamentations 3:22-23

> Repent! Turn away from all your offenses; then sin will not be your downfall. Rid yourselves of all the offenses you have committed, and *get a new heart and a new spirit.*
>
> Ezekiel 18:30-31, italics added

You need a new heart. You need to commit to live by grace and mercy. You need to entrust your life and family to God's design and desire (i.e., His Word). No matter the cost to your pride and temporary happiness, you need to follow in His steps, while at the same time teaching and modeling "the way to life" for others.

> He who heeds discipline shows the way to life,
> but whoever ignores correction leads others astray.
>
> Proverbs 10:17

What have you taught and modeled to those around you? In your response to pain, injustice, and difficulties have you "shown the way to life" or have you led others astray? What would your friends say? How about your spouse? How would your children describe your patterned responses to conflict and offenses?

What have you taught and modeled to those around you?

No matter what has happened in the past, you can break the cycle of pain and destruction. How can this be done? "Get rid of all bitterness, rage and anger, brawling and slander, along with every form of malice" (Eph 4:31). How do we get rid of *all* bitterness? The next verse tells us: "Be kind and compassionate to one another, forgiving each other, just as in Christ God forgave you" (Eph 4:32).

What is more, we need to establish a new, deeper, and permanent example. We need to follow a godly pattern. We need to know and live out God's love. Simply put, we need to live as Jesus lived.

> Be imitators of God, therefore, as dearly loved children and live a life of love, just as Christ loved us and gave Himself up for us as a fragrant offering and sacrifice to God.
>
> Ephesians 5:1-2

> *Train yourself to be godly.* For physical training is of some value, but godliness has value for all things, holding promise for both the present life and the life to come.
>
> 1 Timothy 4:7-8, italics added

A forgiving family is a loving and functional family. Mercy and grace are the keys to functioning in life, as well as to a godly, faithful, and loving family.

The wonderful news is that no matter what has happened up until this point in your life, you can introduce God's grace and mercy into your family right now. It must start with you! You cannot wait for, or depend on, someone else to change, repent, or be the one to introduce forgiveness. The responsibility lies with *you*; and, therefore, there is hope!

Jesus teaches and commands that you take the initiative in conflicts, forgiveness, and reconciliation:

> Therefore, if you are offering your gift at the altar and there remember that your brother has something against you, leave your gift there in front of the altar. First go and be reconciled to your brother; then come and offer your gift.
>
> Matthew 5:23-24

If you are married, the first place to begin is with your spouse. If you have been severely lacking in grace, then your life, your marriage, and your family will be blessed beyond measure by your decision to live a new life in accordance with God's desire.

If you have children that are still under your roof and authority, then the impact of God's truth and mercy applied from this day forward will prepare and equip those children for life.

> Train a child in the way he should go,
> and when he is old he will not turn from it.
>
> Proverbs 22:6

You cannot wait for someone else to change, repent, or be the one to introduce forgiveness.

Responsibility lies with you; and, therefore, there is hope!

How you handle grace and mercy NOW will heavily impact every relationship you have in the future.

The teaching of the wise is a fountain of life,
turning a man from the snares of death.

Proverbs 13:14

For you know that we dealt with each of you as a father deals with his own children, encouraging, comforting and urging you to live lives worthy of God, who calls you into His kingdom and glory.

1 Thessalonians 2:11-12

If you are single, now is a wonderful time to prepare your heart for your future relationships. Do not wait until your spouse and kids arrive. "Dig down deep" *now* so that you can lay your foundation on the Rock (Lk 6:46-49). How you handle grace and mercy *now* will heavily impact every relationship you have in the future.

If you are a parent and have been bitter and caused pain, you have no idea how much you may bless and impact your children now if you *truly* seek their forgiveness. Many people that I know or have counseled long to hear their mom and/or dad genuinely seek their forgiveness for the specific hurtful things they have done.

Incredible fruit can come from the repentant words, "I am so sorry. Please forgive me for…," especially when these words are said by mom or dad. Incredible healing. Incredible restoration. Incredible reconciliation. Incredible newness of life. Incredible love! Incredible blessings!

If you are willing to say that you love your children, then you must back this up with "actions" and "truth" (1 Jn 3:18). "Greater love has no one than this, that he lay down his life for his friends" (Jn 15:13). As parents, we must be willing to lay down our selfishness, our pride, our stubbornness, and humbly seek forgiveness from our children where needed. If you are not willing to do this, then you absolutely must reconsider how much you really love your children!

Before talking to them, you may need to spend some time considering all that you have done to hurt your children. All of us, as parents, have done things that have hurt our children. There are no perfect parents. Yet, try to focus on the bigger and more painful issues rather than the minor ones. If you are not sure what these are, then openly ask your children for specific offenses that they are aware of.

All of this must be done with the right motive. No one appreciates false contrition. No one likes self-justification ("I'm sorry, *but…*"). No one likes "worldly sorrow." No one likes half-hearted attempts to deal with deep wounds. If you are overly defensive and not genuinely ready to repent and seek forgiveness, then it's better that you don't attempt it until you are. Most likely, you will only compound the problem and make it more painful than it was to begin with.

Remember that phrases such as, "I'm sorry if you were hurt," or, "I'm sorry if you had a painful childhood," and, "I'm sorry, *but…*" tend to add insult to injury. Be specific! Don't make excuses. Don't blame other people or things. Take full responsibility for what *you*

We must be willing to seek forgiveness from our children where needed.

If you are not willing to do this, then you absolutely must reconsider how much you really love your children!

No one likes half-hearted attempts to deal with deep wounds.

have done, no matter what the circumstances. Check for signs of godly sorrow, described in the following way:

> See what this godly sorrow has produced in you: what earnestness, what eagerness to clear yourselves, what indignation, what alarm, what longing, what concern, what readiness to see justice done.

2 Corinthians 7:11

When your heart/motive is ready, pursue this life-changing encounter with your children (and, in time, with all others). It will be uncomfortable—there is no way around it. But your faithfulness to God, the pursuit of truth, and your love for your children will more than make it worth your temporary discomfort. Love will do no less than this. And as a result of your obedience to God, there will be endless possibilities for fruitful and loving relationships with your children!

Imagine the far-reaching effects of parents introducing mercy and grace to their families, of parents being the starting point for reconciliation with their children? Think of how many people this would impact! If the reconciled children would then take God's grace and mercy to their families, and so on, and so on… Try to conceive of the influence this would have on our society, the church, and the world.

> You are the light of the world. A city on a hill cannot be hidden. Neither do people light a lamp and put it under a bowl. Instead they put it on its stand, and it gives light to everyone in the house. In the same way, let your light shine before men, that they may see your good deeds and praise your Father in heaven.

Matthew 5:14-16

As daunting as this may sound, it all starts with you and your faithfulness to God's design and desire. If you can establish forgiveness, repentance, humility, and joy in your family, you will potentially impact the lives of thousands, if not millions! Yet, more precisely, you can begin by blessing the lives of those closest to you. *You* are the perfect place to start!

> A cheerful look brings joy to the heart,
> and good news gives health to the bones.
> He who listens to a life-giving rebuke
> will be at home among the wise.
> He who ignores discipline despises himself,
> but whoever heeds correction gains understanding.
> The fear of the Lord teaches a man wisdom,
> and humility comes before honor.

Proverbs 15:30-33

Imagine the far-reaching effects of parents introducing mercy and grace to their families and how many people this would impact!

It all starts with you and your faithfulness to God's design and desire.

A Beautiful Life

- List the names of the people with whom you will commit to introducing God's design and desire for grace and mercy.

31

ANATOMY OF AN OFFENSE

When someone hurts you…

You feel pain, pain that God *specifically* and *intentionally* allowed in your life. That pain and the resulting anger and/or grief are purposely designed by your Maker. These things are intended to motivate you to do something about the problem as well as other possible problem-patterns in your life. Do not let the pain and the offending person control you (e.g., self-pity, gossip, victim-hood, depression)!

> An offended brother is more unyielding than a fortified city, and
> disputes are like the barred gates of a citadel.
>
> Proverbs 18:19

When someone hurts you, the pain that you experience informs you of what you already (should) know…that the offender is a self-centered sinner (just like you) who, at least from time to time, thinks of himself before he thinks of God and others. Inevitably, when just one person acts selfishly, many others will be hurt.

> For where you have envy and selfish ambition, there you find disorder
> and *every evil practice*.
>
> James 3:16, italics added

Being hurt by someone confirms, yet again, that life is not fair. The offense is another reminder that your hope is not in the performance of people, in the things of the world, or in this life, but, in God and eternity (Ps 37; 62; 73; Matt 6:21, 33; Jn 6:27; 7:37-38; Heb 10:32-36). Our hearts are such that we need frequent reminders to store up treasures in heaven, not on earth.

> Whom have I in heaven but you?
> And earth has nothing I desire besides you.
>
> Psalm 73:25

When you experience pain, it also verifies another adage: Life is hard! You *will* suffer repeatedly in this life (Prov 3:11-12; Jn 16:33; Phil 1:29; 1 Pet 4:1-2, 12-14).

Do not let the pain and the offending person control you.

When just one person acts selfishly, many others will be hurt.

There is no avoiding pain. It will find you out. The real question is not how much pain, but, rather, how will you *handle* the pain, injustice, unfairness, offense, etc. when it happens (Matt 5:38-48; Heb 12:11c)? Is your life or "house" built on the rock or on the sand (see Matt 7:24-27; Lk 6:46-49)? Your response to the offense and the resulting experience will reveal what it is that you have built your life on.

> Remember how the LORD your God led you all the way in the desert these forty years, to humble you and *to test you in order to know what was in your heart*, whether or not you would keep his commands.
>
> Deuteronomy 8:2, italics added

An offense exposes your own weaknesses and absolute need for Christ (Deut 8:2-3; 2 Chr 32:31; Lk 8:13), while driving you toward Jesus (2 Cor 1:8-9) and His Word (Ps 119:67, 119:71). At the same time, an offense teaches you, once again, that Jesus (His grace) is totally sufficient for you.

> But he said to me, "*My grace is sufficient for you*, for my power is made perfect in weakness." Therefore I will boast all the more gladly about my weaknesses, so that Christ's power may rest on me. That is why, for Christ's sake, I delight in weaknesses, in insults, in hardships, in persecutions, in difficulties. For when I am weak, then I am strong.
>
> 2 Corinthians 12:9-10, italics added

An offense reminds you that all people, especially the offender, need continual mercy, grace, forgiveness (see Heb 12:15a), understanding, compassion, and love…just as you need and have received from Jesus.

An offense reveals your character (Ex 20:20; Deut 8:2; 2 Chr 32:31). It uncovers both your weaknesses and strengths. What is important or highly valued by you is accurately disclosed (Heb 4:13; Matt 6:21). Your desires and motives (Jas 4:1-3), whether selfish or godly, self-seeking or Kingdom-seeking, are clearly unveiled. An offense tells you precisely what you need to change!

An offense ushers in temptation. When we are hurt, we are often tempted to gossip, dwell in self-pity, and exact revenge. Usually, the first instinct of our flesh is to strike back and inflict pain on the offender, often with more severity than the original offense. But, if we give in to our fleshly feelings, we will experience escalating conflicts, deeper problems, and ever-increasing pain. However, it is important to remember that the fact that we are confronted with the pattern of the world and the passion of our flesh is not, in itself, a sin or failure. Everyone experiences this temptation, as did Jesus Himself (Heb 4:15). It is our *response* to the temptation that matters.

With all of these things in mind, let's look at some of the specific *opportunities* that an offense provides.

Your response to the offense and the resulting experience will reveal what it is that you have built your life on.

An offense reveals your character.

It tells you precisely what you need to change.

Every offense gives you the opportunity to:

- **Change Your Heart**
  You have an opportunity bursting with chances to transform and radically change your heart.

  (See Matt 7:3-5; Col 3:1-2; Heb 12:10-11; 1 Pet 1:6-9, 3:15.)

- **Fulfill Scripture**
  An offense is the perfect opportunity to fulfill Jesus' words by losing your life so that you will find it in Him.

  (See Lk 9:23-24; Jn 12:25.)

- **Influence Others for Jesus**
  You come to a fork in the road where you can make any painful situation a stumbling block or a stepping stone. You can willingly incarcerate yourself into a chamber of continuous torture, or you can give and re-live the same grace, mercy, love, blessings, compassion, and gift that you undeservedly and abundantly received from Christ Himself. While you can never change the heart of another, you can make an unforgettable impact by loving like Jesus loved you.

  (See Matt 5:13-16; Heb 12:15.)

- **Be Conformed to the Image of Jesus**
  Most importantly, but also most often forgotten and neglected...you *get to* please, love, and glorify God, no matter how the other person responds. In so doing, you are being conformed more and more to the image of Christ.

  (See Rom 8:28-29, 12:1-2; 2 Cor 3:18.)

When an offense occurs, how you will respond is always your choice alone. Let's look at the first and best scenario. If you have chosen wisely (the way of love and truth), you can say with the psalmist:

> I have chosen the way of truth;
> I have set my heart on your laws.
>
> Psalm 119:30

> Therefore everyone who hears these words of mine and puts them into practice is like a wise man who built his house on the rock. The rain came down, the streams rose, and the winds blew and beat against that house; yet it did not fall, because it had its foundation on the rock.
>
> Matthew 7:24-25

Ideally, from selfless and godly love will come loving *confrontation*. Confrontation, when carried out in a loving way, will hopefully bring about *confession*. Confession will preferably lead to *repentance*, including the asking for and granting of specific *forgiveness* for

You come to a fork in the road where you can make any painful situation a stumbling block or a stepping stone.

While you can never change the heart of another, you can make an unforgettable impact by loving like Jesus loves you.

You GET TO please, love, and glorify God, no matter how the other person responds.

specific offenses. If properly followed by both parties, this biblical model will ultimately result in *reconciliation* of the relationship and glory to God.

If you choose to love, then, depending on the circumstances (Rom 12:18; Heb 12:14), you must confront the other person with his words/behavior/sin (Lk 17:3; Gal 6:1; 2 Tim 2:25). And, it is worth repeating, this must be done in love! We are to speak the truth in love (Eph 4:15; 1 Cor 13:6), not so much for our benefit or happiness (Rom 15:1), but for the benefit of the offender, other people, and God (Eph 4:29; Mk 12:30-31).

Remember, your job is not to change the other person—it is to love him. Change is *a* goal, but love is *the* goal. If your desire/motive is anything less than love, you will experience the fruit of this in your own life (usually worry and anger), as well as in your relationships. Your hope should be *in God alone* as He chooses to work in the life of the other person. Your hope is not in the other person or yourself. Your sole responsibility is to be faithful to God's desire and design (Ps 33:16-22).

> He who conceals his sins does not prosper,
> but whoever confesses and renounces them finds mercy.
>
> Proverbs 28:13

In a perfect world, the offender would confess every time when confronted with a real sin. But this, unfortunately, is the exception rather than the rule.

However, if the offender was to confess (Prov 28:13; Ps 32:1-5; 1 Jn 1:9), ideally he would take the next step and truly repent ("renounce" the undesired conduct and change his thinking, behavior, and heart out of "godly sorrow" and love; 2 Cor 7:10-11; Lk 3:8). This response, regrettably, also tends to be a rarity.

If the offender is confronted with the truth in love, and he confesses his transgression and truly repents, then he should take it to the next level and seek your forgiveness. While there is a shortage of reaching this level, it does happen. In fact, the more you practice love, the more you will appreciate and experience all that goes into this process.

An "apology" or an "I'm sorry if you were hurt," does not cut it. You must be sincere and *specific* in your confrontation, confession, repentance, and especially in seeking forgiveness. If you stole $1,000 last Friday, then you need to confess, repent, and seek forgiveness explicitly for stealing $1,000 last Friday. Do not say or accept something along the lines of, "I'm sorry if I did something that might have hurt you in some kind of way." Who wants to hear that? How helpful, loving, responsible, or repentant is that kind of attitude? It is more of a slap in the face than it is helpful, and it is a prime example of "worldly sorrow" (2 Cor 7:10), rather than one of being genuinely humble, repentant, and loving.

If and when you are able to lovingly advance to this stage, then it is your turn again. You "get to" forgive the specific offense(s) that the offender committed. When you do this, you are re-living God's mercy and grace that He generously gave to you. Try to consciously think about God's gift to you when you are forgiving another.

Your job is not to change the other person—it is to love him.

Change is A goal, but love is THE goal.

You must be sincere and SPECIFIC in your confrontation, confession, repentance, and especially in seeking forgiveness.

Be kind and compassionate to one another, forgiving each other, just as in Christ God forgave you.

Ephesians 4:32

By truly forgiving, you have become more like God and less like the world. You have chosen to walk by faith and love rather than temporary gratification and the "Fairness Doctrine." You have stored up treasures and glory in heaven rather than here on earth. You have been and will continue to be truly blessed by God (Matt 6:19-21; 1 Cor 3:12-15; 2 Cor 3:5-18, 4:16-18).

When all of this is accomplished (by both parties), growth and improvement in your relationship should follow. You both will have successfully loved each other through a painful, difficult, and often unpleasant process. God, His desire and design, and the other person will have been put above your selves (Phil 2:1-4; 2 Cor 5:15; Jas 4:10). Each of you will know the other's character and love far more than before the offense occurred. Further, as a result of having loved one another biblically, your relationship, overall, will most likely be better than it was to begin with.

Offenses are clear opportunities to love and grow in your relationships. Yet, it always comes down to how *you* decide to handle the offenses.

If, for countless reasons, the process falls through at any stage, it is still your responsibility to forgive. It is wonderful when the other person confesses, repents, etc., but do not set your hope on these things happening. Neither does your forgiveness of the other person depend on them (Matt 6:12, 14-15; Mk 11:25).

On the other hand, when confronted with an offense, if you refuse to forgive, you have chosen the way of the world (1 Cor 1:18-21; Rom 12:2; Jas 4:4) and the way of the flesh (Gal 5:17, 6:7-8; 2 Pet 2:10). By refusing to forgive anyone, you will experience more and more separation from God (Matt 6:14-15) and the fruit that comes with it, including poor relationships, depression, despair, loneliness, bitterness, worry, a critical, judgmental heart, etc. (Hos 10:13; 2 Cor 7:10b; Gal 6:7-8; Eph 2:3; Jn 10:10a). If you refuse to forgive, in light of all you know, you have chosen foolishly.

But everyone who hears these words of mine and does not put them into practice is like a foolish man who built his house on sand. The rain came down, the streams rose, and the winds blew and beat against that house, and it fell with a great crash.

Matthew 7:26-27

However, with God and His grace, our failures, weaknesses, and sin do not mean that all is lost. Yet another opportunity to exercise forgiveness will afford itself to you (Rom 5:20; 2 Cor 12:9-10; Jas 4:6; Rev 2:4-5). Look for where you went wrong (Matt 7:3-5; Lk 9:23-24; Rom 8:5-8; 1 Cor 13:1-7; 1 Jn 4:16-19), repent (Ezek 18:30; Acts 20:21; 2 Cor 7:10-11), and start anew according to God's desire and design (Mk 12:30-31; 1 Cor 14:1; 2 Cor 5:15-17; Gal 5:6; 1 Pet 4:8; 1 Jn 4:16).

Repeat this process until you have loved, forgiven, and glorified God.

By truly forgiving, you have become more like God and less like the world.

Offenses are opportunities to love and grow in your relationships.

If the process falls through at any stage it is still your responsibility to forgive.

What will you choose?

Now what I am commanding you today is not too difficult for you or beyond your reach. It is not up in heaven, so that you have to ask, "Who will ascend into heaven to get it and proclaim it to us so we may obey it?" Nor is it beyond the sea, so that you have to ask, "Who will cross the sea to get it and proclaim it to us so we may obey it?" No, the word is very near you; it is in your mouth and in your heart so you may obey it.

See, I set before you today life and prosperity, death and destruction. For I command you today to love the Lord your God, to walk in his ways, and to keep his commands, decrees and laws; then you will live and increase, and the Lord your God will bless you in the land you are entering to possess.

This day I call heaven and earth as witnesses against you that I have set before you life and death, blessings and curses. Now choose life, so that you and your children may live and that you may love the Lord your God, listen to his voice, and hold fast to him. For the Lord is your life.

Deuteronomy 30:11-16, 19-20, italics added

"The word is very near you; it is in your mouth and in your heart so you may obey it."

Deuteronomy 30:14

A Beautiful Life

Illustration of the right way and the wrong way to handle an offense:

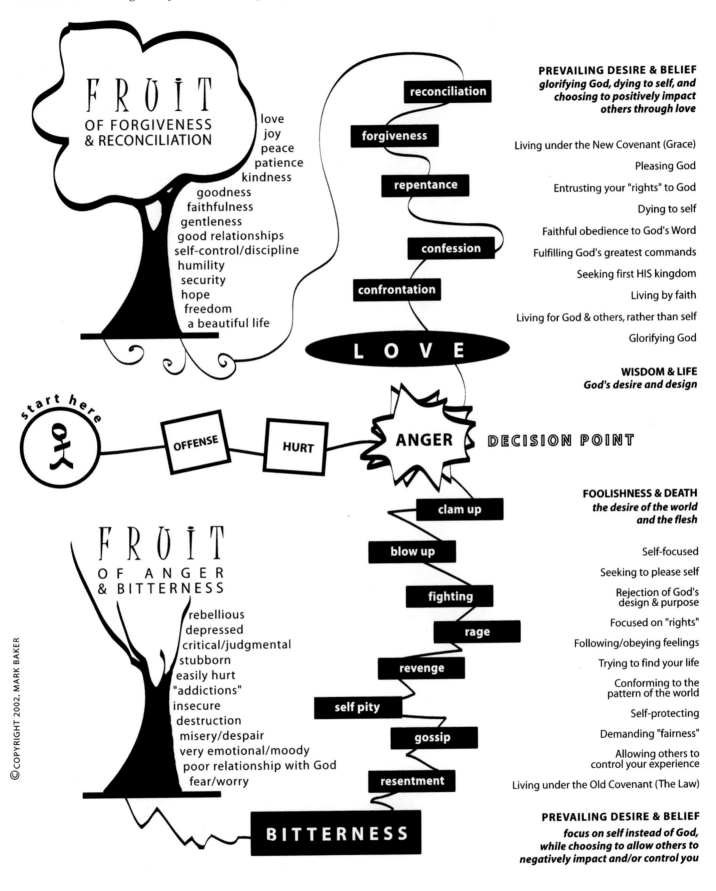

FRUIT
OF FORGIVENESS
& RECONCILIATION

love
joy
peace
patience
kindness
goodness
faithfulness
gentleness
good relationships
self-control/discipline
humility
security
hope
freedom
a beautiful life

reconciliation

forgiveness

repentance

confession

confrontation

LOVE

PREVAILING DESIRE & BELIEF
glorifying God, dying to self, and choosing to positively impact others through love

Living under the New Covenant (Grace)

Pleasing God

Entrusting your "rights" to God

Dying to self

Faithful obedience to God's Word

Fulfilling God's greatest commands

Seeking first HIS kingdom

Living by faith

Living for God & others, rather than self

Glorifying God

WISDOM & LIFE
God's desire and design

start here

OFFENSE HURT ANGER DECISION POINT

FRUIT
OF ANGER
& BITTERNESS

rebellious
depressed
critical/judgmental
stubborn
easily hurt
"addictions"
insecure
destruction
misery/despair
very emotional/moody
poor relationship with God
fear/worry

clam up

blow up

fighting

rage

revenge

self pity

gossip

resentment

BITTERNESS

FOOLISHNESS & DEATH
the desire of the world and the flesh

Self-focused

Seeking to please self

Rejection of God's design & purpose

Focused on "rights"

Following/obeying feelings

Trying to find your life

Conforming to the pattern of the world

Self-protecting

Demanding "fairness"

Allowing others to control your experience

Living under the Old Covenant (The Law)

PREVAILING DESIRE & BELIEF
focus on self instead of God, while choosing to allow others to negatively impact and/or control you

A Beautiful Life

- In which areas of godly conflict resolution are you weak?

- Which areas of conflict are your strengths?

- Which specific conflicts do you need to address after finishing this book?

- What can you do to grow in your specific weaknesses?

32

CONCLUSION

Now all has been heard;
Here is the conclusion of the matter:
Fear God and keep his commandments,
For this is the whole duty of man.
For God will bring every deed into judgment,
Including every hidden thing,
Whether it is good or evil.

Ecclesiastes 12:13-14, italics added

As clearly demonstrated, instead of endless pain and bitterness, your life can be filled with opportunities, growth, grace, mercy, love, fruit of the Spirit, godly relationships, reconciliation, beauty, and glory to God. And all of these things do not depend on circumstances or other people, but on your desire for what God desires. So the question must be asked: what is it that you truly want? What is it that you truly live for, fight for, and would even die for? What are you willing to do with all of the truth you have learned?

Further, what good is your will if it is against God's will? What good is God's Word without faith and obedience? What good is wisdom if you cherish the world and its folly? What good is pain if you don't learn and grow from it? What good is truth if you do not trust it? What good is love without commitment, actions, and truth? What good is God to you if you don't need Him, know Him, love Him, or hope in Him? How much hope is to be found in dwelling on, and living in, the past? What good is the key to freedom if you insist on remaining enslaved? What is life without forgiveness?

We can be like the stubborn and wicked servant, or we can be like the sinful, yet humbled, forgiven, loved, forgiving, and loving woman. We can be tortured and stunted by our past, like Frank, or we can be free and at peace, like Mary, displaying a truly beautiful life—the natural result of a forgiving heart.

We are all called to imitate and walk like Jesus in love and grace. And if He calls us, He has fully equipped us. Contrary to what we may think, people and circumstances do not dictate our experience. Our trust in, and obedience to, God and His Word is always the overriding issue.

> **What is it that you truly want?**

> **People and circumstances do not dictate our experience. Our trust in, and obedience to, God and His Word are always the deciding factors.**

How have you handled the offenses, unfairness, injustices, and pain in your life? Are you still searching for your life in this fallen world? Is your hope still in the performance of sinful people? Do you see or are you blind to the opportunities that afford themselves through offenses, conflict, and hurt? Are your life and relationships marked by the Old Covenant or the New? In what areas have you fallen for a bogus gospel?

No one is saying that forgiveness is easy (it does, however, become easier). But it is exceedingly more difficult and painful to *not* forgive. Throughout this book, you have seen what God's Word says regarding your absolute need to forgive others. You now know what you need to know, and you have all the power and strength that is necessary to act on that knowledge. The determining factor is your will. "Do you want to get well?" (Jn 5:6) Or do you want to remain a victim—tortured and imprisoned? Is holding on to your pride and the pity you receive from others worth the rejection of God's desire and design? Or will you believe and live out the reality of *His* kingdom come, *His* will be done (Matt 6:10)?

If you believe in God's desire and design and if you are willing, then write your name in the following pledge as a loving commitment before God to remain in Him (Jn 15:1-17) and in His New Covenant:

> "I, _____ , hereby do gladly agree and commit to living by grace, love, freedom, forgiveness, and God's power, while, just like Christ, entrusting all my rights, unfair treatment, and circumstances, good and bad, over to God. Unfairness, mistreatment, offenses, and injustices are now divine opportunities to re-live God's love, grace, and mercy; to impact others for the kingdom of God; to grow and mature; to conform to the image of Christ; and to glorify God. My hope is no longer in the performance of sinful man or in the corrupt ideas and desires of the world but in the perfect character of God."

The determining factor is your will.

Do YOU want to get well?

A Beautiful Life

- In what specific ways will your life be different from now on?

- *How* will you go about effecting these changes?

- *When* will you make these changes?

- *Why* will you make these changes?

APPENDIX A

We need to forget what we do not need to remember, at the same time that we remember, focus on, and meditate upon the God-ordained essentials of life.

First, what does God's Word say about forgetting?

> Forget the former things;
> *do not dwell on the past.*
> See, I am doing a new thing!
>
> Isaiah 43:18-19, italics added

> But one thing I do: Forgetting what is behind and straining toward what is ahead, I press on toward the goal to win the prize for which God has called me heavenward in Christ Jesus.
>
> Philippians 3:13-14

> "Do not
> dwell on
> the past."
>
> Isaiah 43:18

What does "forget" mean, in the context of forgiveness?

> **FORGET:** Do not pursue; do not dwell on; put out of your mind completely.

What specific things should you forget?

- *Forget* **THE PAST**
  Which includes the following:

    - **"What is behind"** (Phil 3:13-14)

    - **Sins of others**
      Whoever and whatever needs to be forgiven

    - **Your own sins**
      Following repentance before God, there is *no* condemnation for those in Christ Jesus…you are free!

- *Forget* **LIVING FOR YOURSELF**
  Always remember…it is *not* about you!

- *Forget* **YOUR RIGHTS**
  Always remember…life is *not* fair; entrust your rights to God.

- *Forget* **THE OLD COVENANT, THE "FAIRNESS DOCTRINE"**
  Living according to performance (yours and others') or dependant on your own strength; you *cannot* live life depending upon yourself. Remember: you are not under the law, but under God's grace (The New Covenant).

- *Forget* **TRYING TO CONTROL WHAT YOU CANNOT CONTROL**
  (i.e., worry); trying to change others and how they treat you.

- *Forget* **WORKING FOR WHAT IS TEMPORARY AND FADING**
  "Do not work for food that spoils, but for food that endures to eternal life, which the Son of Man will give you" (Jn 6:27a).

- *Forget* **THE WORLD'S PROMISES**
  They are lies that lead to destruction.

- *Forget* **EVERYTHING THAT IS FALSE**
  Counterfeits, lies, and deception are all around us (see *Chapter 25* regarding the "bogus gospel").

- *Forget* **THE PURSUIT OF "HAPPINESS"**
  Attempting to be "happy" and "fulfilled" in the world and outside of God (i.e., idolatry).

- *Forget* **FOLLOWING YOUR DECEITFUL AND CORRUPT DESIRES**
  These come from your sinful nature (i.e., turning people, things, happiness, and pleasure into idols).

- *Forget* **PUTTING YOUR HOPE IN THE PERFORMANCE OF PEOPLE**
  Do not misplace your hope. "Cursed is the one who trusts in man, who depends on flesh for his strength and whose heart turns away from the LORD" (Jer 17:5, see also Ps 73:25).

- *Forget* **MAN'S "WISDOM" OR THE WORLD'S "WISDOM"**
  (Gen 3; 1 Cor 1, 2) A little truth mixed with a lot of lies.

Always remember… it is NOT about you!

You CANNOT live life depending upon yourself.

Along with forgetting, what does God's Word say about remembering?

> So I will always remind you of these things, even though you know them and are firmly established in the truth you now have. I think it is right to refresh your memory as long as I live in the tent of this body.

2 Peter 1:12-13

What does "remember" mean, in the context of forgiveness?

REMEMBER: Meditate upon; dwell on; apply, live, cherish.

What specific things should you remember?

- *Remember* **TO GLORIFY GOD IN** *ALL* **THAT YOU DO**
  Your goal should be to please God and to *love* Him.

- *Remember* **TO "KNOW AND RELY ON" GOD'S LOVE FOR YOU**
  This love God has for us is perfect, all-powerful, life giving, and abundant (1 Jn 4:16).

- *Remember* **YOU HAVE BEEN GIVEN FULLNESS IN CHRIST**
  God and His love are abundantly more than you need.

- *Remember* **THE GREATEST COMMAND**
  To *love* the Lord your God and to *love* your neighbor.

- *Remember* **WHAT COUNTS**
  Absolutely nothing you do in life "counts," unless it is done "through love" (Gal 5:6).

- *Remember* **WITHOUT HIM, YOU ARE NOTHING**
  Without His love you are nothing, have nothing, know nothing, can do nothing, and you remain in darkness and death.

- *Remember* **THE GOAL: LOVE**
  While a change in others and the situation may be *a* goal, it is not *the* goal. It is not your job to change others or manipulate circumstances; you are called to love.

- *Remember* **WHAT YOU DESERVE**
  You deserve death, hell, and God's wrath (Rom 3:23, 6:23; Eph 2:4).

- *Remember* **WHO YOU ARE**
  Your standing in life is based solely on the mercy, grace, and love of God, not on your goodness, works, intelligence, upbringing, etc.

Your goal is to please God and to LOVE Him.

God and His love are abundantly more than you need.

You deserve death, hell, and God's wrath.

- *Remember* **TO IMITATE JESUS**
  Through forgiveness, you are imitating the character of Jesus. Forgiveness is always subject to the offended person's character, not the worthiness of the offender.

- *Remember* **THE INEVITABILITY OF BEING OFFENDED**
  You *will* be hurt, offended, betrayed, unfairly treated, and experience injustice for the rest of your life. It is how and why you respond that matters most.

- *Remember* **YOUR PRIORITY**
  Life is always a matter of priorities, of which there is really only One (Ps 27:4; Matt 6:33; Lk 10:42; 2 Cor 8:5).

- *Remember* **TO BE THANKFUL**
  Remember to be thankful, always, for God's perfect character and the wonderful gifts He freely and generously gave you and will continue giving to you: His love, blessings, salvation, forgiveness, life, mercy, grace, hope, faithfulness, power, truth.

- *Remember* **THE *JOY* OF YOUR SALVATION**
  Remember the joy of your salvation; in so doing, you can freely forgive, just as you have been forgiven. A truly grateful heart will always lead to a forgiving person.

- *Remember* **GOD'S DESIGN**
  Forgiveness is God's design to transplant your hope from the performance of people to the glory of God! Forgiveness always draws us closer to Jesus. Unforgiveness always drives us away from Jesus (Matt 6:14-15; Job 5:2).

- *Remember* **YOUR HOPE IS IN GOD *ALONE***
  There is *no hope* outside of God. Everything is hopeless apart from Him (Rom 15:4, 15:13; Ps 62).

- *Remember* **THE BIG PICTURE**
  Remember that there is always more to the picture than what we can see. We must live in the light of eternity, "fixing our eyes on what is unseen" (2 Cor 4:18) and on "the life to come" (1 Tim 4:8).

- *Remember* **IT IS *NOT* ABOUT YOU**
  You are called to live for *God* and *others…not* yourself! (2 Cor 5:15; Lk 9:23-24; Mk 12:30-31)

- *Remember* **LIFE IS NOT FAIR, AND IT NEVER WILL BE**
  Nor should you want it to be. You must stop putting your hope in the idea of fairness!

- *Remember* **THE NEW COVENANT**
  You need to live this life depending completely upon God and according to His grace…*not* yourself, not others, and not in the hope of fairness.

> You WILL be hurt, offended, betrayed, unfairly treated, and experience injustice for the rest of your life.
>
> It is how and why you respond that matters most.

> Remember the joy of your salvation.

> There is NO HOPE outside of God.

A Beautiful Life

- *Remember* **WITHOUT FAITH, EVERYTHING IS SIN**
  Without faith, it is impossible to please God. The *only* thing that counts is faith expressing itself through love.

- *Remember* **FAITHFULNESS DETERMINES EXPERIENCE**
  The life you experience is determined by your faithfulness to God's design and desires.

- *Remember* **GOD'S WORD**
  God's Word gives you "everything" you "need for life and godliness" (2 Pet 1:3; see also Deut 6:6-9; Josh 1:8; Ps 1:1-3; 19; 119:61, 83, 93, 109, 141; Prov 7:1-3).

- *Remember* **GOD'S PROMISES**
  He is *perfect*! He *never* fails. He *always* keeps His Word! (2 Pet 1:3-4; 2 Tim 3:15-17)

- *Remember* **EVERYTHING THAT IS TRUE**
  More specifically: Jesus (truth is a person; Jesus is the Word).

- *Remember* **THE LORD YOUR GOD**
  "Do this in remembrance of Me" (1 Cor 11:23-26).

- *Remember* **TO PRAY CONTINUALLY**
  "Devote yourselves to prayer, being watchful and thankful" (Col 4:2; see also 1 Thes 5:17; Rom 1:9, 10; Phil 4:6-7).

- *Remember* **GOD'S WORD OF ENCOURAGEMENT**
  "The Lord disciplines those He loves" (Heb 12:5-11).

- *Remember* **THE TRUE NATURE OF "TROUBLES**
  Your troubles are "light and momentary" and are achieving an "eternal glory" (2 Cor 4:16-18).

- *Remember* **YOUR RESPONSIBILITY**
  You are called to be a good steward of the many things that God has given you (Matt 25:14-30).

- *Remember* **YOU WILL SOMEDAY SEE JESUS FACE-TO-FACE**
  You will have to give an account to God for what you did in this life. How incredible would it be to hear Him say to you, "Well done, good and faithful servant"?

> The life you experience is determined by your faithfulness to God's design and desires.

APPENDIX B

FREQUENTLY ASKED QUESTIONS

Included here are answers to a few of the questions often heard when dealing with the subject of forgiveness.

What if I can't forgive myself?

This question is a prime example of the world's "wisdom" influencing the church. Many Christians and churches teach this decidedly unbiblical idea. However, there is not a single verse in all of Scripture that even hints at a need to forgive ourselves. What should this biblical silence tell us?

If our omnipotent and all-knowing God knew that this would be such an important issue for people, then wouldn't there would be an abundance of Scripture encouraging and exhorting us to play offender, offended, and judge all at this same time? Yet, there is not a single verse or example in the Bible which speaks of this unnecessary, deceptive, and diversionary notion.

In actuality, when someone feels a need to forgive one's self, the problem is generally that he does not fully grasp and/or appreciate God's grace. For him, whether practically or emotionally, God's grace is perceived as insufficient to deal with the sin in his life. Yet to all of us, God says, "My grace is sufficient for you" (2 Cor 12:9).

Another problem associated with the idea of forgiving one's self stems from a failure to truly repent of the sin in question. Even though we rarely change overnight, true repentance means that we turn away from, and stop doing, the sin in question. If, instead, we repeatedly keep committing the sin, we will continually feel guilty and construe from this that the feelings of guilt mean that we need something else (e.g., self-forgiveness).

In reality, earnest confession, true repentance, and faith in God's unlimited grace are all anyone needs when it comes to being forgiven. This is the New Covenant! Forgiving your *self*, on the other hand, is a myth at best, and destructive at worst.

> Forgiving your SELF is a myth at best, and destructive at worst.
>
> Earnest confession, true repentance, and God's unlimited grace are all anyone needs when it comes to being forgiven.

If I forgive, won't I become a "doormat,"
allowing others to abuse or take advantage of me?

Remember that forgiveness comes under the umbrella of love. It is not just forgiveness or unforgiveness that is at stake when we are hurt or offended by another. The ultimate dilemma is to love or not to love. Forgiveness is a smaller, but notably significant, subset of the greater reality of love.

Is it loving God and the repeat offender if you allow the offender to abuse you and/or to take advantage of you? Are you helping him by allowing his sinful behavior? His sin is absolutely unacceptable and, in love, must be addressed. *Not* to do so is unloving!

Many people confuse love with what has been labeled "enabling," "co-dependency," or "acceptance." Pretending that everything is okay, rescuing a person time and time again from the consequences of his sin, "believing the best" in someone despite the harsh reality of his behavior, hoping everything will just "work out," covering up the sin, keeping up appearances, etc., are all common examples of these worldly mindsets that are decidedly **not**, by Scripture's definition, loving. In fact, these destructive behaviors reside on the other end of the spectrum of true love, and are not loving at all. Many times the outcome of such "love" is worse than hatred!

Consider the wisdom of Scripture and its forceful contradiction of the worldly ideas and behaviors listed above…

> He who spares the rod *hates* his son,
> but he who loves him is careful to discipline him.
>
> Proverbs 13:24, italics added

> Discipline your son, for in that there is hope;
> *do not be a willing party to his death.*
>
> Proverbs 19:18, italics added

> A hot-tempered man must pay the penalty;
> *If you rescue him, you will have to do it again.*
>
> Proverbs 19:19, italics added

> Do not withhold discipline from a child;
> if you punish him with the rod, he will not die.
> Punish him with the rod
> and save his soul from death.
>
> Proverbs 23:13-14

The ultimate dilemma is to love or not to love.

Are you helping the repeat offender by allowing their sinful behavior?

"You were to Israel a forgiving God, though you punished their misdeeds."

Psalm 99:8

A Beautiful Life

Love should always be the primary and overarching goal in any situation that we find ourselves. If we say that we love God, we cannot refuse to forgive. Forgiveness is never optional. At the same time, we should not think that giving mercy means that we are allowing and accepting sinful and destructive behavior. When offended, hurt, or abused, we must always ask, "What can I do that is loving toward God and the other person?" Forgiving others is always a part of love, yet there are many other aspects (often difficult) to God's desired response from us (i.e., love).

There is "tough love," where we make a difficult decision that will result in undesired consequences in the eyes of the loved one/offender. This is also referred to biblically as discipline, rebuke, and correction (Prov 6:23, 12:1, 13:24, 19:18, 22:15, 23:13; Heb 12:5-11; Rev 3:19). Love may be a literal or figurative spanking. It may be calling the police on an abusive husband, or a teenager high on drugs. You may forgive the personal offense but, in love, allow the offender, for *his* sake, to experience the consequences of his sin (Ecc 8:11; Gal 6:7-8).

We are putting our hope solely in God and His design when we give discipline and/or allow a loved one to experience the necessary outcome of his sin. In order to do this we need faith! In discipline we must always walk by faith and not by sight. Our hope cannot be in our ability, feelings, intellect, or the "goodness" of others. We must trust God alone.

Forgiving someone does not mean you allow, accept, or condone his sinful behavior—it is just the opposite. The popular yet misunderstood terms of "acceptance" and "unconditional love" do not quite square with Scripture. If God's love has no conditions then there would be no hell. Yet many will be separated from God and experience His wrath for all eternity precisely because of His conditions. God loves the whole world, yet not every person will benefit from His love. Some, by rejecting His conditions, will never know God or His love.

God is love. It is His character to love. This does not change. God's love is "unconditional" in that He still loves us when we sin, but God's love *does* have conditions. He loves us *enough* to rebuke us, to correct us, to convict us, to forcefully tell us that our behavior is unacceptable. He loves us so much that our sin is never acceptable. His love never turns a blind eye to sin! If we want to love others like God loves us then we must be willing to confront their sin.

Forgiveness without wisdom is not love. Forgiveness without love is not wise. We must be wise in handling offenses (see Jas 3:13-18; Matt 18:15-20). Love must dictate our decisions and actions, even if it intentionally inflicts pain on the loved one (discipline). God definitely "disciplines us for our good" (Heb 12:10). So should we to others, even if it is difficult or makes us uncomfortable. Our motivation should always be to love God and others no matter what the outcome.

You may forgive the personal offense but, in love, you allow the offender, for his sake, to experience the consequences of his sin.

Forgiveness without wisdom is not love.

Forgiveness without love is not wise.

A FORGIVING HEART
A BEAUTIFUL LIFE

www.hopeink.net
email: hopeink@sbcglobal.net